ENDORSEMENTS

ISRAEL,
THE CHURCH,
AND THE
LAST DAYS

ISRAEL,
THE
CHURCH,
AND THE
LAST DAYS

BY DAN JUSTER AND KEITH INTRATER

Destiny Image® Publishers, Inc.
P.O. Box 310
Shippensburg, PA 17257-0310

"Speaking to the Purposes of God for This Generation
and for the Generations to Come"

ISBN 0-7684-2187-X
(formerly published as 1-56043-061-3)

For Worldwide Distribution
Printed in the U.S.A.

This book and all other Destiny Image, Revival Press, MercyPlace,
Fresh Bread, Destiny Image Fiction, and Treasure House books are available
at Christian bookstores and distributors worldwide.

For a U.S. bookstore nearest you, call **1-800-722-6774**.
For more information on foreign distributors, call **717-532-3040**.
Or reach us on the Internet:
www.destinyimage.com

CONTENTS

Books may be ordered from Destiny Image or directly from Tikkun International. For further information write:

Tikkun International
P.O. Box 2997
Gaithersburg, MD 20866

Tikkun International is committed to the salvation of Israel through congregational planting and the restoration of the Body of Christ.

Send for the companion volume: *The Book of Revelation, the Passover Key*

INTRODUCTION

by Daniel Juster

Keith Intrater and I have been colleagues for eleven years. For the last five years, due to Keith's planting a new congregation, we have lived in different cities. Less time was available for interaction. Last summer, since we were both inspired to teach on the Last Days in our summer Bible school, we decided to team teach. We were amazed to discover that God had led us to the same conclusions on most key issues! This is by the work of the Spirit. This book is a product of that course.

Because the book has two authors some material overlaps, but it is expressed in different ways and in different contexts. This will serve as confirmation! Most material in this book is complementary and dovetailing. As presently laid out, it fits together as pieces of a puzzle.

Keith Intrater's strength is in greater detail and insight into the State of Israel and the Last Days. My strength is in the overall perspective and in relating it to various tribes and movements in the Church (historically and in the present). This will become clear as you proceed.

Please read with an open mind and weigh the biblical evidence since this book puts together several emphases that we believe must come together.

First of all, **this book is restorationist**. We believe in the restoration of the Body of Christ in the Last Days, a restoration of unity, power, gifts of the Spirit, and fivefold ministry. We try to make this clear throughout.

Secondly, **we believe in a key role for Israel** in Last Days events and her reengrafting into the olive tree (see Rom. 11). This role includes the importance of establishing a saved remnant of Israel.

Thirdly, **we are Kingdom of God oriented**. We believe the Kingdom of God has broken into this world through Jesus and His people. Signs, wonders, deliverance, healing, and living by Kingdom principles, as applied to all realms of life, are all part of our witness—although the Kingdom will not come in fullness until Jesus returns. We now preach the Gospel of the Kingdom.

Lastly, **we are premillennial** in its historic pre-1830 form, as taught by George Ladd. This should not be a barrier to our amillennial friends in the other areas we teach. Our teaching, for the most part, transcends this distinction. However, we believe that a premillennial understanding is best for reasons we put forth, so we ask our amillennial friends to be open on this score.

Our Last Days view combines tribulation, glory, and victory for God's people.

We trust this book will inspire you to practical success in extending God's Kingdom rule and in godly living!

CHAPTER 1

AN INTRODUCTION
TO END-TIMES PROPHECY

by Daniel Juster

Two Approaches to Prophecy

The doctrine of the Last Days is crucial for our practical life, Christian walk, and spiritual warfare in the days to come because we must be prepared for what is shortly to take place in the world.

There are two predominant views on the Last Days. One is known as a Reformed perspective. It has its roots in the Reformed, Presbyterian, and Lutheran churches. Some years ago, this view made a renewed appearance in the charismatic world in a movement called "Kingdom Now." Most of those involved in this movement could be called Reformed in theology. They hold to certain ways of approaching the Scriptures. Two views have been common: either that the imminent return of Jesus will immediately lead to the new heavens and new earth, or that the Church will succeed in evangelizing the whole world, which will submit to Jesus before His return. This last view is known as the postmillennial view.

The other predominant viewpoint concerning the Last Days is known as the Dispensational view. Most American Christians are brought up with a dispensational understanding. The word *dispensation* comes from "dispense." In this context it means God dispenses His grace in different ways in different ages.

Most dispensationalists teach that the Body of believers is to be raptured out of the world before the Great Tribulation. Only then will the Tribulation begin. They hold that the Last Days Tribulation has to do primarily with Israel, not the Body of believers.

The dispensationalist makes a very strong distinction between the Old Testament (the dispensation of law) and the New Testament (the dispensation of grace).

Adherents of these two views have been debating for more than 130 years. In America, Reformed theology is espoused by Westminster Theological Seminary in Philadephia. The dispensational viewpoint is espoused by Dallas Theological Seminary. The dispensational viewpoint is seen in the *Scofield Study Bible*, the *Ryrie Study Bible*, and the *Dake Annotated Reference Bible*. The Reformed perspective is somewhat reflected (though not exclusively) in the *NIV Study Bible*.

The Kingdom of God in Dispensationalism

One of the key concepts of the Last Days is the Kingdom of God. The dispensational movement holds that the Kingdom of God refers mostly to the earthly rule of the Messiah in an age of peace. Their teaching roughly follows these lines: When Jesus came He offered the Kingdom to Israel, but Israel rejected the Kingdom. Therefore, the Kingdom was postponed, and God inserted a "Parenthetical Church Age" that was not foreseen by the prophets. This church age will end when the Rapture takes place. At that time the Kingdom of God will be preached again. The gospel that was preached by Jesus and His disciples, known as "the Gospel of the Kingdom," is not the same gospel that believers preach today. We are not to preach the Gospel of the Kingdom. We preach "the Gospel of the grace of God." The two are different. When the Church is taken away in the Rapture, the remnant of 144,000 Jews, mentioned in Revelation 7, will again preach the

Gospel of the Kingdom. This good news is that the earthly Kingdom of God is about to dawn. Messiah will reign for a thousand years. This understanding of the Kingdom relegates almost everything to the future.

In dispensationalist circles, one never preaches "the Kingdom of God," but "the Gospel of God's grace." One does not talk about extending the Kingdom of God. The phrase "the Kingdom of God" refers to a future age of peace. Our own view lies in great contrast to this.

The Interpretation of Prophecy

How shall we respond to historic interpretations? First let us note some principles. The purpose of the doctrine of the Last Days in the Bible is that God's people might know how to order their lives as they see the unfolding of His plan. It is crucial, in understanding the Last Days, to immerse your life in God's purpose. You will thus become a catalyst for seeing God's purpose for the world fulfilled.

The Bible is the means by which we test what we believe the Spirit is revealing to us doctrinally. We cannot build doctrine on what we think the Spirit is saying. We must test it by what the Bible says.

The teachings of the Bible are based on what is called "author's intent." We know that the Holy Spirit is the author of the Scripture, but He is the author of Scripture through men who were inspired by God (2 Tim. 3:16).

The whole Bible is breathed out by God, but it is breathed out by men who spoke in the language that a community of people understood at the time that biblical writer was writing. Each man wrote according to the meaning of the words at that time. The scriptural meaning then depends on the intent of the human author (whose meaning was the same as God's). Unless God said, "Write

15

these words, although you will not know what you are writing," we must assume that the author's meaning is the same as God's.

In general, the biblical writer wrote from the context of a nation besieged, Israel in trouble, the Body of believers under persecution, etc. That context and the languages of Hebrew and Greek provide a meaningful foundation for understanding a text.

Most people would rather not grapple in the Spirit with the intended meaning of a particular text. If you ignore author-intended meaning, however, you can say that you believe the Bible is the test of doctrine all you want, but it will be meaningless because you will be allowing yourself the freedom to go to the Bible and find anything you want to find. The Bible could then say whatever you want it to say.

The Holy Spirit can use the Bible to speak many things to you. The Bible can be a jumping-off point for God to speak to you about your own life, your own personal situation, or your own congregation. That is not the author-intended meaning of the text. This would be the Holy Spirit using the text to speak to you about something. When you are building a doctrinal understanding, however, you must build upon the author-intended meaning of the text.

Israel's Prophets
Their Unique Purpose and Perspective

The prophets of Israel were a unique breed of people. They have often been called "prophets of doom and gloom." There was always a reason for what they said, however, and for the way they said it. They were people of insight and foresight, by the Holy Spirit. They saw a people violating God's Law. They knew that Law to be part of God's covenant in ancient Israel. Knowing the principles of God's covenant, they were aware that the violation of the covenant would lead to judgment. It would lead to Israel's scattering. It would lead to other nations overrunning and destroying Israel.

In the year 586 B.C. the Babylonians marched into Israel and wiped out the last vestiges of that nation. The early prophets foresaw this destruction decades and even centuries in advance. The context of most of the prophets of Israel looks toward this judgment. The post-exilic prophets, Zechariah, Haggai, and Malachi, look back to this judgment. The earlier prophets saw into the future and saw the invading nations as instruments of judgment.

First, Assyria destroyed the northern kingdom, taking the ten northern tribes into captivity from 722 to 701 B.C.

The prophets foresaw the sins of the southern kingdom, Judah: her idolatry, her immorality, her giving herself to the ways of the world. This would bring God's judgment.

The prophets foresaw Jerusalem falling to the Babylonians. They saw the temple being destroyed. This occurred from 600 to 586 B.C.

Habakkuk cried out to God concerning the injustices of Israel's neighbors: "God, why don't You do something?"

God answered, "I will do something. I will send the Babylonians to destroy the land."

"No, not that!" Habakkuk said. "That is not what I had in mind. The Babylonians are unjust. They are idol worshipers. How could You allow them to destroy a nation which is more righteous?"

Solomon's huge temple was so magnificent it was considered one of the wonders of the ancient world. It was the center of life for the Jewish people.

The kingdom that Solomon developed was an empire, the mightiest in the region. Yet the prophets saw it all being wiped out because of sin. They foresaw that God would begin afresh with a remnant.

As the prophets foresaw calamitous events, they called forth judgments. Whether they were simply speaking what God was about to do or whether their words actually initiated the process makes no difference. God's words would not return to Him void. The prophets spoke, and what they spoke happened.

Some of the prophets actually lived through the periods of devastation they prophesied. Yet all of God's prophets looked forward to Israel coming back to the land and being reestablished as a nation. They looked forward to an age in which God's purposes for Israel would be fulfilled. They saw that purpose of God as bringing the world to His knowledge. They foresaw a time in which His justice and love would be poured down upon the earth, and the whole world would be under His rule!

Peace on Earth Through the Messiah

In this context, we can better understand passages such as Isaiah 2:2-4. In the midst of judgment and devastation, the prophets universally foresaw a day of world peace in which the Law would go forth from Jerusalem and the word of the Lord from Zion. The whole world would come under the rule of God and learn peace instead of war.

In the midst of devastation, Isaiah foresaw a glorious age in which the nations would beat their swords into plowshares and their spears into pruning hooks! *"Nation will not take up sword against nation, nor will they train for war anymore."* He could foresee God establishing His Law, not as legalism, but as His covenant principles.

A shoot will come up from the stump of Jesse; from his roots a Branch will bear fruit. Isaiah 11:1

Isaiah prophesied in the days of the Davidic monarchy. He saw the house of David as a stump because the Davidic king would no longer rule. After the Babylonian captivity there would be no more Davidic kings until the one great descendant of David, the Messiah.

18

The Spirit of the LORD will rest on him—the Spirit of wisdom and of understanding, the Spirit of counsel and of power, the Spirit of knowledge and of the fear of the LORD and he will delight in the fear of the LORD. He will not judge by what he sees with his eyes, or decide by what he hears with his ears. Isaiah 11:2-3

This is a prophecy of Yeshua. It predicts His supernatural discernment and the gift of the Holy Spirit upon Him.

But with righteousness he will judge the needy, with justice he will give decisions for the poor of the earth. He will strike the earth with the rod of his mouth; with the breath of his lips he will slay the wicked. Righteousness will be his belt and faithfulness the sash around his waist. The wolf will live with the lamb, the leopard will lie down with the goat, the calf and the lion and the yearling together; and a little child will lead them.

Isaiah 11:4-6

I want you to observe two things: First, this Messiah, this Lord, the rod or the stem of Jesse, shall strike the earth with the rod of His mouth. This sounds very much like the Book of Revelation where we read about the sword coming forth from the mouth of Yeshua and slaying the wicked (Rev. 19). Yeshua will destroy the wicked and bring judgment on the earth. After the judgment, however, "the wolf shall dwell with the lamb, the leopard shall lie down with the young kid, the calf and the young lion and the fatling together." Obviously the whole order of nature will be changed in this glorious age. The prophets foresaw this time.

The cow will feed with the bear, their young will lie down together, and the lion will eat straw like the ox. The infant will play near the hole of the cobra, and the young child put his hand into the viper's nest. They will neither harm nor destroy on all my holy mountain, for the earth will be full of the knowledge of the Lord as the waters cover the sea. In that day the Root of Jesse will stand as a banner for the peoples; the nations will rally to him, and his place of rest will be glorious. In that day the Lord will reach out his hand a second time to reclaim the remnant that is left of his people from Assyria, from Lower Egypt, from Upper Egypt, from Cush, from Elam, from Babylonia, from Hamath and from the islands of the sea.   Isaiah 11:7-11

Isaiah continues in this vein:

He will raise a banner for the nations and gather the exiles of Israel; he will assemble the scattered people of Judah from the four quarters of the earth.   Isaiah 11:12

This verse connects world redemption with the regathering of the Jewish people. It speaks of an age in which the nations will come to the knowledge of God, an age in which all the world will know God. There will be peace on earth and a whole new order of nature. Fierce animals will no longer be dangerous. The phrase that thrills my heart most is the one that says:

They will neither harm nor destroy on all my holy mountain, for the earth will be full of the knowledge of the LORD as the waters cover the sea.   Isaiah 11:9

Knowledge in the Old Testament has to do with an intimate relationship with God. This intimate communion with God would cover the earth as the water covers the sea. I believe the implication here is that the whole world would be baptized with the Holy Spirit.

The prophet foresaw God's purpose in Israel fulfilling her role as servant, to usher in world redemption. The purpose of Israel as a nation was somehow connected to the establishment of

God's Kingdom and Law over all the earth. The knowledge of the Lord would cover the earth.

God's Kingdom, the Ultimate Hope of the Prophets

When we talk about the Last Days, we must begin with the perspective of the ultimate hope of the prophets. The ultimate hope of the prophets was the worldwide knowledge of God, the establishment of God's Law over the entire earth, and the establishment of God's Kingdom in fullness. The words we have read are an ample description of it.

God's Kingdom is the rule of God. Wherever God is ruling, that is where His Kingdom is. Where God is ruling in fullness, His Kingdom manifestation is full. The prophets looked beyond the devastating periods of judgment to an age in which God's rule would be fully manifested on the earth. The Kingdom of God is tied up with God's principles being lived out. God's love is established, God's government is established, and the whole order of everything changes. That is the Kingdom of God. Again we note it is preceded by judgment.

> *The earth is broken up, the earth is split asunder, the earth is thoroughly shaken. The earth reels like a drunkard, it sways like a hut in the wind; so heavy upon it is the guilt of its rebellion that it falls—never to rise again. In that day the LORD will punish the powers in the heavens above and the kings on the earth below. They will be herded together like prisoners bound in a dungeon; they will be shut up in prison and be punished after many days.* Isaiah 24:19-22

God's judgment will precede the coming of His Kingdom in fullness. Joel spoke a parallel word. We also find the same picture in the Book of Revelation. It is a picture of worldwide judgment. The leaders of rebellious nations will be punished.

The Removal of Veils

According to Isaiah 24:23, the judgment will be followed by the reign of the Lord.

On this mountain the LORD Almighty will prepare a feast of rich food for all peoples, a banquet of aged wine—the best of meats and the finest of wines.　　　Isaiah 25:6

This passage concerns Mount Zion, Israel, and Jerusalem. I see nothing in its context to imply that it means the Church, though we could apply it by analogy.

On this mountain he will destroy the shroud that enfolds all peoples, the sheet that covers all nations. Isaiah 25:7

Paul declared to the Romans that a veil lies over the eyes of the Jewish people. He told the Corinthians that the faces of the Jewish people are veiled when they read the Hebrew Scriptures. But it is not only the Jewish people that are veiled; all the nations that do not believe are veiled as well. The Lord has promised to destroy that veil. In other words, something will happen in Israel that will be part of God's destroying the veil that keeps all men from receiving truth. This will result in the redemption of the whole world!

The Redemption of the Whole World

According to the predominant church traditions in America today, the end of this age will culminate with most of the world going to hell. When Jesus returns, it will be too late for repentance. In dispensational premillennial teaching, the millennial age will be a time for God to demonstrate His judgment. There will be world peace only because He rules with a rod of iron. Salvation is out of the question, however. It will be too late. He is calling out a saved people only during this age.

In amillennial teaching, the return of the Messiah leads to the judgment of all peoples without a literal millennial age. Again, most people are lost.

The heart of God spoken through the prophets is so much more optimistic! His intention is that Israel will bring the whole world to the knowledge of God. The veil will be removed from all nations. The Kingdom will come in fullness.

> *Turn to me and be saved, all you ends of the earth; for I am God, and there is no other....Before me every knee will bow; by me every tongue will swear. They will say of me, "In the LORD alone are righteousness and strength." All who have raged against him will come to him and be put to shame. But in the LORD all the descendants of Israel will be found righteous and will exult.* Isaiah 45:22-25

The word that has gone out of God's mouth and which shall not return to Him void is a word of world redemption. Philippians 2 reveals Yeshua leaving His Father's throne, descending to earth and becoming like us. There we read that every knee shall bow and every tongue confess that Jesus is Lord (vv. 10-11). This passage is based on Isaiah 45. This clearly shows the divinity of Yeshua because in Isaiah 45 it says that at the holy name of God, Yahweh, every knee shall bow and every tongue confess.

I was taught that this verse describes the Great White Throne Judgment of Revelation 20. When all unsaved humanity stands before God before being cast into hell, each one would be forced to bow the knee and acknowledge the lordship of Yeshua. However, when taken in context, this is not the true meaning. The meaning is that an age is coming in which the whole world will acknowledge God and in which the knowledge of God will cover the earth as the waters cover the sea. The wolf will lie down with the lamb.

Every knee shall bow and every tongue will confess or take an oath. They will say, *"It is surely in the Lord that I have righteousness and strength."* In other words, everybody in the whole world will confess Jesus as their righteousness. What an optimistic hope about the ultimate destiny of humanity! All of humanity is to be saved, not lost. Is this heresy? Or is this what God's Word proclaims?

The Redemption of All Israel

We have already quoted Isaiah 45; let us look at some other Scriptures that show a greater optimism.

> *But I said, "I have labored to no purpose; I have spent my strength in vain and for nothing. Yet what is due me is in the LORD'S hand, and my reward is with my God." And now the Lord says—he who formed me in the womb to be his servant to bring Jacob back to him and gather Israel to himself, for I am honored in the eyes of the Lord and my God has been my strength.* Isaiah 49:4-5

This is Yeshua's role in bringing Israel back to God. To think that Israel will not ultimately be saved is wrong.

> *This is what the LORD says: "In the time of my favor I will answer you, and in the day of salvation I will help you; I will keep you and will make you to be covenant for the people, to restore the land and to reassign its desolate inheritances."* Isaiah 49:8

Yeshua is our covenant with God. Paul declared that all Israel would be saved (Rom. 11:26). Some people think this is not fair. Israel, however, is the representative nation among the nations in this verse. The Church, the Body of believers, is only metaphorically a nation. It is really a people gathered from all nations, Jews and Gentiles. But Israel is a nation literally. When we read that all

Israel will be saved, Israel is being given a representative role. The implication is that all France will be saved, all Germany will be saved, etc. This is the fullness of the prophetic hope. The salvation of Israel is interconnected with all the nations coming to the knowledge of God. The salvation of Israel and the salvation of the nations is spoken of together.

Salvation for Israel and the Nations

This is what the Sovereign Lord says: "See, I will beckon to the Gentiles, I will lift up my banner to the peoples; they will bring your sons in their arms and carry your daughters on their shoulders."   Isaiah 49:22

This speaks of a time in which Israel and the nations will be reconciled. The nations which come to the knowledge of God will be so excited about Israel as God's historic people that they will carry them back into the land. These nations will bow down to Jesus.

He put on righteousness as his breastplate, and the helmet of salvation on his head; he put on the garments of vengeance and wrapped himself in zeal as in a cloak. According to what they have done, so will he repay wrath to his enemies and retribution to his foes; he will repay the islands their due. From the west, men will fear the name of the LORD, and from the rising of the sun, they will revere his glory. For he will come like a pent-up flood that the breath of the LORD drives along.
             Isaiah 59:17-19

This speaks about the ultimate salvation of Israel. God's judgment leads to the spread of the knowledge of God (v. 19).

"The Redeemer will come to Zion, to those in Jacob who repent of their sins," declares the LORD.   Isaiah 59:20

This is the verse that Paul quotes in Romans 11:26.

"As for me, this is my covenant with them," says the LORD. "My Spirit, who is on you, and my words that I have put in your mouth will not depart from your mouth, or from the mouths of your children, or from the mouths of their descendants from this time on and forever," says the LORD. Isaiah 59:21

This is the ultimate salvation of Israel from generation to generation. Isaiah continued to reflect upon this age of salvation for Jew and Gentile:

For this is what the LORD says: "I will extend peace to her like a river, and the wealth of nations like a flooding stream; you will nurse and be carried on her arm and dandled on her knees. As a mother comforts her child, so will I comfort you; and you will be comforted over Jerusalem." When you see this, your heart will rejoice and you will flourish like grass; the hand of the LORD will be made known to his servants, but his fury will be shown to his foes. See, the LORD is coming with fire, and his chariots are like a whirlwind; he will bring down his anger with fury, and his rebuke with flames of fire. For with fire and with his sword the LORD will execute judgment upon all men, and many will be those slain by the LORD. Isaiah 66:12-16

Arise, shine, for your light has come, and the glory of the LORD rises upon you. See, darkness covers the earth and thick darkness is over the peoples, but the LORD rises upon you and his glory appears over you. Nations will come to your light, and kings to the brightness of your dawn. Isaiah 60:1-3

I don't believe that anyone who has rejected the Lord will be saved or that this salvation for the whole earth includes everyone who ever lived. It rather includes the survivors of the Last Days. Isaiah shows us the conclusion of it all:

I will send some of those who survive to the nations—to Tarshish, to the Libyans and Lydians (famous as archers), to Tubal and Greece, and to the distant islands that have not heard of my fame or seen my glory. They will proclaim my glory among the nations. And they will bring all your brothers, from all the nations, to my holy mountain in Jerusalem as an offering to the LORD.... "As the new heavens and the new earth that I make will endure before me...so will your name and descendants endure. From one New Moon to another and from one Sabbath to another, all mankind will come and bow down before me," says the LORD. "And they will go out and look upon the dead bodies of those who rebelled against me; their worm will not die, nor will their fire be quenched...."   Isaiah 66:19,20,22,24

This salvation ultimately includes Israel and the nations. In the same passage we see a worldwide recognition of the Sabbath and the new moon. On the one hand we see great judgment; on the other hand we see the whole world coming to the knowledge of God.

The New Covenant and the Age to Come

The New Covenant promises the worldwide Kingdom of God in its connection to Israel. God makes His covenant with the nations through Israel. The Noahic covenant was the last one made directly to the nations. Jeremiah prophesied:

*"The time is coming," declares the LORD, "when I will
make a new covenant with the house of Israel and with
the house of Judah."* Jeremiah 31:31

The context in which we see this New Covenant is the glorious age he is talking about. The meaning of the New Covenant is the fullness of the Kingdom of God in the age to come. Jeremiah 31:34-37 connects this Kingdom clearly to the nation of Israel. God's Law is established in righteousness. The evidence of the New Covenant is the establishing of God's Law!

Several other passages speak of the New Covenant either directly or by clear implication. They speak for themselves.

*And afterward, I will pour out my Spirit on all people.
Your sons and daughters will prophesy, your old men
will dream dreams, your young men will see visions.
Even on my servants, both men and women, I will pour
out my Spirit in those days. I will show wonders in the
heavens and on the earth, blood and fire and billows of
smoke. The sun will be turned to darkness and the moon
to blood before the coming of the great and dreadful day
of the LORD. And everyone who calls on the name of the
LORD will be saved; for on Mount Zion and in Jerusalem
there will be deliverance, as the LORD has said, among
the survivors whom the LORD calls.* Joel 2:28-32

The Judgments Precede Redemption

Peter quoted this passage on the Day of Pentecost as the Spirit was poured out on his company in Jerusalem (Acts 2:17-19). Judgment and the plagues of the Exodus, however, become the pattern for the prophetic description of later judgment and for the description of judgments in the Book of Revelation (where they are basically a repetition of the Exodus plagues—on a worldwide scale and at a much greater level of intensity). Israel and the Body of believers will experience a greater exodus than crossing through the sea.

The prophets used such terms as "the shaking of the heavens" and "the sun turning to darkness" to describe events of their day. The Day of the Lord has to do with God's visitation in judgment and salvation. The prophet looked at the day in which he lived, a day of judgment, as the Day of the Lord. The Day of the Lord was also seen as the ultimate day of judgment, salvation, and visitation.

Paul quoted Joel 2:32 in Romans 10. After the great judgment, whoever calls on the Lord shall be saved. Joel shows the judgment of all the nations for the sake of Israel.

> *In those days and at that time, when I restore the fortunes of Judah and Jerusalem, I will gather all nations and bring them down to the Valley of Jehoshaphat. There I will enter into judgment against them concerning my inheritance, my people Israel, for they scattered my people among the nations and divided up my land.*
>
> *Joel 3:1-2*

Revelation 14 repeats the same theme. The concept of the winepress of God's wrath is repeated in Isaiah 63:3 and Revelation 19:15.

> *"Let the nations be roused; let them advance into the Valley of Jehoshaphat, for there I will sit to judge all the nations on every side. Swing the sickle, for the harvest is ripe. Come, trample the grapes, for the winepress is full and the vats overflow—so great is their wickedness!" Multitudes, multitudes in the valley of decision! For the day of the LORD is near in the valley of decision. The sun and moon will be darkened, and the stars no longer*

shine. The LORD will roar from Zion and thunder from Jerusalem; the earth and the sky will tremble. But the LORD will be a refuge for his people, a stronghold for the people of Israel. "Then you will know that I, the LORD your God, dwell in Zion, my holy hill. Jerusalem will be holy; never again will foreigners invade her. In that day the mountains will drip new wine, and the hills will flow with milk; all the ravines of Judah will run with water. A fountain will flow out of the LORD'S house and will water the valley of acacias."   Joel 3:12-18

Judgment Is Followed by Salvation

These great judgments or shakings lead to Israel's salvation and the worldwide Kingdom.

The LORD will be king over the whole earth. On that day there will be one LORD, and his name the only name. The whole land, from Geba to Rimmon, south of Jerusalem, will become like the Arabah. But Jerusalem will be raised up and remain in its place, from the Benjamin Gate to the site of the First Gate, to the Corner Gate, and from the Tower of Hananel to the royal winepresses. It will be inhabited; never again will it be destroyed. Jerusalem will be secure. This is the plague with which the LORD will strike all the nations that fought against Jerusalem: Their flesh will rot while they are still standing on their feet, their eyes will rot in their sockets, and their tongues will rot in their mouths. On that day men will be stricken by the LORD with great panic. Each man will seize the hand of another, and they will attack each other. Judah too will fight at Jerusalem. The wealth of all the surrounding nations will be collected—great quantities of gold and silver and clothing. A similar plague will strike the horses and mules, the camels and donkeys, and all the animals in those camps. Then the survivors from all the nations that have attacked Jerusalem will go up year after year to worship the King, the LORD Almighty, and to celebrate the Feast of Tabernacles. If any of the peoples of the earth do not go up to Jerusalem to worship the King, the LORD Almighty, they will have no rain. If the Egyptian people do not go up and take part, they will have no rain. The LORD will bring on them the plague he inflicts on the nations that do not go up to celebrate the Feast of Tabernacles. This will be the punishment of Egypt and the punishment of all the nations that do not go up to celebrate the Feast of Tabernacles.

Zechariah 14:9-19

The First-Century Jewish Context

In the first century the Jewish people were saturated with this prophetic hope. They believed there was coming an age on earth, brought into being by the Messiah, that would lead to the fulfillment of this glorious prophecy. They did not know when the resurrection would occur. They believed the Messiah would come and destroy the enemies of Israel as described in these passages. After the destruction of Israel's enemies, God, through His Messiah, would establish a worldwide age of peace.

They were looking for the Messiah, who would come and deliver them from their enemies. Through the glory He would pour out upon Israel, and through their deliverance, not only Israel but the whole world would come to the knowledge of the Lord. They would see the dawning of the hope of all the prophets; the knowledge of the Lord would cover the earth as the waters cover the sea; the Law would go forth from Zion. They would see the Spirit poured out on all flesh so that the worldwide knowledge of God would be established. There would be great prophecy; there would be abundance in nature. Nothing would hurt or destroy in all God's holy mountain. The Lord would be one over all the earth. Idolatry would cease, and everybody would worship the God of Israel as the one true God, the Creator of heaven and earth.

The nation of Israel was carried off into Babylonian captivity. Then, seventy years later, a remnant returned to rebuild the temple. Since the majority of the Israelites left in the land were from Judah, those other remnants joined with them to make one new nation. But most of the Jewish people remained in the Babylonian area. The Diaspora, the scattered Jewish people, have been the majority of Jewry since 586 B.C. The regathering in fullness never took place. In the days of Jesus, a few million Jewish people lived in the land of Israel, but the majority remained outside of Israel.

Israel had once again lost its sovereignty and was ruled by the Romans. The king imposed upon them was King Herod. He was only partially of Jewish descent, an Edomite. He built a great temple. However, since the return from Babylon, Israel had passed through five hundred years without a king. Many times she had been mocked and attacked by her enemies. The Jewish people cried out to God to intervene and save them from this Roman oppression. Inspired by the prophets, they had not lost the hope of a glorious future.

The prophetic hope of the redemption of Israel and the world was still the great desire of the Jewish people. When John the Baptist announced the Kingdom of God, the Jewish people understood that the fulfillment of that hope was near. Great excitement and anticipation spread throughout the land. However, the fullness of the hope of the Kingdom did not come upon earth, at least not as anticipated. Our next chapter will address the meaning of the coming of the Kingdom of God. In what sense did the Kingdom come? In what sense is the Kingdom, the prophetic hope, yet to be fulfilled?

CHAPTER 2

THE GOSPEL OF THE KINGDOM AND THE LAST DAYS

by Daniel Juster

The prophets looked forward to a time when world redemption would take place and the earth would transition from this age to the age to come. However we understand that age to come, the hope of the prophets was nothing less than this: The people of God would so fulfill their destiny that the knowledge of the Lord would cover the earth as the waters cover the sea.

A Summary of the Prophetic Hope

1. That age, as we described it, is summarized by the following: Israel will be delivered from her enemies.

2. The Gentiles or the nations will come to the light of God.

3. The Spirit will be poured out upon all flesh. This is a parallel way of describing the Isaiah 11 promise that the knowledge of the Lord will cover the earth. A prophetic gift will be restored worldwide, and an age of glorious peace will reign. The wolf will lie down with the lamb; the nations will beat their swords into plowshares and their spears into pruning hooks; and nations will not learn war anymore. There will be safety on earth. Children will

play near the viper's den and the cobra's hole. They will not hurt in all God's holy mountain.

4.   The New Covenant, whereby the Law will be written upon the heart of the people of God, will be universally applied. God's people will be moved to obey His statutes and judgments (Ezek. 36).

The prophets agree that God's purpose is to establish His justice and righteousness throughout the whole earth. God's concern has always been that His laws, His ways, or His principles would be established among mankind worldwide. We read in Isaiah 2 that the word of the Lord will go forth from Jerusalem, that the Law will go forth from Zion. We read concerning the Messiah in Isaiah 42 and 49 that He will not rest until He establishes the Law of God on the earth.

The Hope Is to Establish God's Law

The grace of the New Covenant, which internalizes the Law, does not do away with the Law. Through the Holy Spirit, the people are finally able to live out the Law of God. The Mosaic Law is an accommodation to some degree to the conditions present at the time it was given. However, in terms of the universal principles of God's Law, it is something to be established in all the earth. There is a Jewish rooting to that ideal age to which we look. All the world will celebrate the Feast of Sukkot. All the world will celebrate the Sabbath and the new moon (Isa. 66).

The prophets understood the age to come as being the age of the Kingdom rule of God. They understood the nation of Israel, when it was faithful to the laws of God, to be a manifestation of the Kingdom of God. However, when they describe the age to come as in Isaiah 2, 11, and 45, they put forth a great hope. Isaiah says that every knee will bow and every tongue will take an oath in the name of the God of Israel. Everyone in the whole world will say, "In the LORD I have righteousness and strength." This was understood as the Kingdom of God in fullness. The Kingdom rule of God is characterized by the prophetic descriptions we just summarized.

The Kingdom of God and John the Baptist

The Kingdom was proclaimed in the preaching of John the Baptist, who came declaring to the people, "Repent, for the kingdom of God is at hand"—(repent that you might enter into the Kingdom; repent that you might be part of it). You can imagine the extraordinary excitement of the people when, after no prophetic voice had been heard for four hundred years, John the Baptist emerged as a prophet.

So when he said, "The Kingdom of God is here," the people thought, "Now we will be delivered from our enemies. Now we will see the judgment of God come on the earth and the nations come to the light of God." They had to repent, therefore, and go through the waters of baptism to prepare themselves to be part of God's mercy and rule rather than be under God's judgment.

The announcement of the coming of God's Kingdom was thrilling news. It implied the coming of the Messiah and His rule.

Then Yeshua came as a prophet. With signs and wonders confirming His word, He also announced the arrival of the Kingdom of God. Surely all those who were not biblically illiterate understood that the proclamation of the Kingdom of God was the announcement, in some way, of the same message of the prophets—the glorious dawning of the age of peace, of the power of God, of worldwide healing, of victory over sin, and of the fullness of the Spirit in which everyone would prophesy.

In the sixth month, God sent the angel Gabriel to Nazareth, a town in Galilee, to a virgin pledged to be married to a man named Joseph, a descendant of David.

The virgin's name was Mary. The angel went to her and said, "Greetings, you who are highly favored! The Lord is with you." Mary was greatly troubled at his words and wondered what kind of greeting this might be. But the angel said to her, "Do not be afraid, Mary, you have found favor with God. You will be with child and give birth to a son, and you are to give him the name Jesus. He will be great and will be called the Son of the Most High. The Lord God will give him the throne of his father David, and he will reign over the house of Jacob forever; his kingdom will never end."   Luke 1:26-33

This signaled the dawning of the Kingdom of God that all had been waiting for. As Zechariah said,

Praise be to the Lord, the God of Israel, because he has come and redeemed his people. He has raised up a horn of salvation for us in the house of his servant David (as he said through his holy prophets of long ago), salvation from our enemies and from the hand of all who hate us—to show mercy to our fathers and to remember his holy covenant, the oath he swore to our father Abraham: to rescue us from the hand of our enemies, and to enable us to serve him without fear in holiness and righteousness before him all our days.   Luke 1:68-75

Did the Kingdom of God Come?

To Miriam and Zechariah, the Kingdom was "now." In other words, it was an accomplished fact. The fact that the Messiah was born meant that God had delivered Israel. Did it happen? Did the Kingdom come? Or didn't it come? How do we put it together? This prophecy must have a broader fulfillment than we have yet seen. Did the Last Days come when Yeshua came? The people who

38

received Him certainly thought so. Were they mistaken? Was the kingdom postponed for two thousand years as the dispensationalists teach? We must look into these questions.

> *Simeon took him in his arms, and praised God, saying: "Sovereign Lord, as you have promised, you now dismiss your servant in peace. For my eyes have seen your salvation, which you have prepared in the sight of all people, a light for revelation to the Gentiles and for glory to your people Israel."* Luke 2:28-32

The deliverance of Israel from her enemies and from the constant distresses that plagued her is announced. The hope of the prophets is announced. The Messiah's role is to save all nations. Messiah was for all nations, but especially the glory of Israel. When He came, men realized that the Last Days were dawning upon them. Deliverance was at their doorsteps.

Did the Kingdom Come?
The Message of Jesus and
the Meaning of the Kingdom of God

Jesus was immersed in the river by John the Baptist. He began to preach where John left off. He said, *"Repent for the Kingdom of God is at hand."* Then He did extraordinary miracles. He healed the sick. He cast out demons. He taught with authority, and not like the scribes and Pharisees.

The scribes and Pharisees taught by quoting ancestral teachers as precedent for their positions. They would say, "So and so taught that," and "So and so taught this. Therefore, the correct interpretation of the Law must be this..." Their authority for doctrine or practice was a consensus.

Yeshua taught the Law without appealing to the rabbinic precedent. He said, *"It has been said* [the common interpretation], *but I say unto you, this is how the Law is applied"* (Matt. 5–7). He taught as none other. He commanded nature with authority. At His command the sea was calmed and fish and bread were multiplied. He fed thousands. He raised the dead.

When the Messiah came to earth, He left His divine power behind. The miracles of Jesus are not proof of His divinity but are the full picture of restored humanity. The authority He demonstrated is the ultimate authority human beings were meant to have, had they not rebelled against God. He is the restoration of the human race. His person represents the greatness in which man could have walked. Man could have avoided natural disaster, disease, and the dangers of evil. This was all part of Jesus' role in the restoration of mankind. As sin and death came through man, so salvation had to come through man. Because God delegated authority on earth to human beings, it is only through human beings filled with His Spirit that the work of God goes forward in the world.

Wonderful things were happening: Miracles were taking place. Demons were fleeing. Nature was being tamed at His feet. Yet Rome was still ruling. The disciples began to get impatient. "It is time to overthrow the Romans; it is time for the judgments to come so that we can see Israel saved and the nations come to the knowledge of God," some must have thought.

When Jesus announced the Kingdom of God, the disciples and others among the Jewish people understood that all those prophetic promises were ready to dawn in fullness.

John the Baptist was the cousin of the Messiah. He expected the deliverance of God to come any day. Instead he found himself sitting in jail. Not only was he sitting in jail, but he was about to lose his head. I try to imagine how he felt in that situation. "Yes, Yeshua looks pretty good, but He certainly isn't doing what I expected the Messiah to accomplish."

*After Jesus had finished instructing his twelve disciples,
he went on from there to teach and preach in the towns
of Galilee. When John heard in prison what Christ was
doing, he sent his disciples to ask him, "Are you the one
who was to come, or should we expect someone else?"*

Matthew 11:1-3

He perhaps was thinking that Yeshua's ministry might have
been just another preparatory ministry. What did it all mean?

The Kingdom Comes in Supernatural Ministry

*Jesus replied, "Go back and report to John what you
hear and see. The blind receive sight, the lame walk,
those who have leprosy are cured, the deaf hear, the
dead are raised, and the good news is preached to the
poor. Blessed is the man who does not fall away on account of me." As John's disciples were leaving, Jesus
began to speak to the crowd about John: "What did you
go out into the desert to see? A reed swayed by the
wind? If not, what did you go out to see? A man dressed
in fine clothes? No, those who wear fine clothes are in
kings' palaces. Then what did you go out to see? A
prophet? Yes, I tell you, and more than a prophet. This
is the one about whom it is written: 'I will send my mes-
senger ahead of you, who will prepare your way before
you.' I tell you the truth: Among those born of women
there has not risen anyone greater than John the Baptist; yet he who is least in the kingdom of heaven is
greater than he."* Matthew 11:4-11

Yeshua describes here, from the Book of Isaiah, the signs of
the Kingdom of God and the age to come which are appearing in
His ministry. "Go tell John the things which you see. Yes, John, I
am the One who was to come. All the characteristics that the

prophets described as pertaining to the Kingdom of God are manifested in My ministry through the Holy Spirit." He gave a description of the signs of the Kingdom of God. The Kingdom of God is manifested when the blind receive their sight, the lame walk, the lepers are cleansed, the dead are raised up, and the poor have the gospel preached to them. Any movement without these signs present is manifesting very little of the Kingdom of God.

It Is Greater to Be in the New Covenant Kingdom

Jesus said something very important to His disciples. Of all the men previously born, the greatest of them was John the Baptist. Was he greater than Isaiah? Jeremiah? Moses? What did Jesus mean? Moses led the children of Israel out of Egypt and brought them to the Promised Land. Why was John the Baptist greater? John the Baptist was greater because he was privileged to be born at the end of the old age, to announce the inauguration of the age to come. He was the forerunner of the Messiah. No greater prophetic role was possible in the old age!

Jesus went on: "*He who is least in the Kingdom of God is greater than John.*" What does that mean? It is not speaking of the status of those who are in heaven or the future Millennium. John will be part of that age to come and will have a place of great honor. Rather Yeshua is speaking of the present reality of the Kingdom. This truth is important to your understanding of this age and the Last Days. Jesus saw Himself standing at the end of the old age on the brink of the age to come that the prophets predicted. To enter into the realities of the new age is greater. In the new age, everyone has access to the Father, everyone can be baptized in the Holy Spirit, and everyone can hear the prophetic voice of God. Everyone can come into the power of the life that Jesus demonstrated. This is greater than the role of John the Baptist. The least person in the Kingdom of God, in this sense, has a greater position than John. This is why the people who lived in the days of the prophets longed to be partakers of that into which we have entered. They lived in a time of preparation, but we have entered into the reality. Yeshua is thus clearly stating that the Kingdom of God has come.

The Kingdom Stage of Gospel Proclamation

" 'We played the flute for you, and you did not dance; we sang a dirge, and you did not mourn'. For John came neither eating nor drinking, and they say, 'He has a demon.' The Son of Man came eating and drinking, and they say, 'Here is a glutton and a drunkard, a friend of tax collectors and "sinners." ' But wisdom is proved right by her actions." Then Jesus began to denounce the cities in which most of his miracles had been performed, because they did not repent. Matthew 11:17-20

The ministry of Yeshua came to a climax when He died on the cross. That certainly was unexpected. I can only imagine the confusion that filled the hearts and minds of the people who accepted Him as the Messiah. Their minds now had to be expanded to a whole different understanding of the Kingdom. They had seen the signs, they had seen the miracles, they had seen the Kingdom of God dawning. They expected these events to lead to the overthrow of Rome and the fulfillment of the prophecy of Zechariah 14, the prayer of Simeon, and the word of the angel. Instead, the Messiah was hanging on a cross! Where did that fit in—if the Kingdom of God had indeed come? They might have been able to live with John the Baptist losing his head, but how could they live with the Messiah dying on the cross?

But he who stands firm to the end will be saved. And this gospel of the kingdom will be preached in the whole world as a testimony to all nations, and then the end

*will come. So when you see standing in the holy place
"the abomination that causes desolation," spoken of
through the prophet Daniel—let the reader understand—
then let those who are in Judea flee to the mountains.
Let no one on the roof of his house go down to take anything out of the house. Let no one in the field go back to
get his cloak. How dreadful it will be in those days for
pregnant women and nursing mothers! Pray that your
flight will not take place in winter or on the Sabbath.*

Matthew 24:13-20

The prophetic hope, the prayers and prophecies of Anna and
Simeon, and the announcement of Gabriel were all accurate. There
was yet another piece to be added to the puzzle.

The same Isaiah who said the Messiah would deliver Israel
from her enemies and be a light to the nations also described the
servant as suffering unto death as a sacrifice for His people. There
is no clear evidence that anybody ever put the whole thing together until after Yeshua rose. Then He showed His disciples what the
Scriptures had foretold. He not only rose from the dead, He went
through walls and appeared and disappeared. He walked and
talked with His disciples for forty days. Then He ascended back to
heaven.

Before He left them again, Yeshua told them, "*Go and wait in
Jerusalem for the promise.*" In obedience they all gathered in the
Upper Room and joined together in prayer. During a prayer meeting on the day of *Shavuot*, the Holy Spirit fell. This was the day
when the Jewish people celebrated the giving of the Law. It is only
by the Spirit that the Law is established in the earth.

The Kingdom Breaks in Through the Spirit

When the Holy Spirit was poured out everyone spoke in other
languages. Peter said it was a fulfillment of the promise of Joel.

"In the last days...I will pour out my Spirit on all people. Your sons and daughters will prophesy, your young men will see visions, your old men will dream dreams. Even on my servants, both men and women, I will pour out my Spirit in those days" (Acts 2:17-18).

If the Spirit was poured out on all flesh, the age to come has dawned. The Kingdom has come. Yet the fullness of the judgment foretold in Joel, the sun being darkened and the moon turning to blood and the signs of fire in the Last Days before the great and terrible day of judgment, have not fully come. The Holy Spirit was made available to all but was not poured out yet "on all flesh."

> *Repent, then, and turn to God, so that your sins may be wiped out, that times of refreshing may come from the Lord, and that he may send the Christ, who has been appointed for you—even Jesus. He must remain in heaven until the time comes for God to restore everything, as he promised long ago through his holy prophets.*
>
> Acts 3:19-21

The restoration of all things is the knowledge of the Lord covering the earth. God spoke this by the mouths of all His prophets since the world began. This passage reflects a truth about the Kingdom of God. The Kingdom had come in part. We can date it from the ministry of Yeshua. It increases by His crucifixion, the resurrection, the ascension, the outpouring of the Spirit, and the combination of the whole. An exact date for its beginning is not that important. What is important is that the New Testament perspective on the Kingdom of God is that the Kingdom really did come in the life and ministry of Jesus and in the reception of the Spirit by His disciples. The age to come did dawn, but it did not come in fullness. The Kingdom of God is already here, but it is not yet here in fullness. *It is already, but not yet.* It is a reality. The Kingdom has come, but it has not come in totality.

That's why Peter said, *"This is that which was spoken by the prophet Joel."* He was saying that the Kingdom had come from the hand of the Lord. He also said, *"And, that God might send Jesus who must remain in heaven until the times of the restoration of all things."* This was to show that the Kingdom of God is yet to come! It has come and it is yet to come. It is here and it is tomorrow. It is now and it is future.

This truth is so essential in Jewish ministry because the primary question Jewish people ask is, "If Jesus is the Messiah, why is the world in such a mess?" The answer to that is, "It isn't in such a mess over here. It is not a mess in my life. It is not a mess in the life of our community." "Maybe it is not a mess for you, but I am dying of cancer," someone might say. Our response may be, "Let me show you the Kingdom of God. I rebuke that cancer. Get out of him!"

That is the manifestation of the Kingdom of God! It has not come in fullness because people are still sick and dying. The age described by the prophets has not yet come in totality, but it has come partially. It comes when families are whole. It comes when marriages are healed. It comes when you create an alternate school that is full of the Spirit instead of sending young people into the jaws of the secular humanistic world. It comes when businessmen prosper in godly principles instead of the ways of the world. After all, are there not going to be businessmen in the millennial age? Will they not prosper by godly principles?

The New Testament view on the Kingdom of God is that the age to come has broken into this age since the death and resurrection of Jesus, His ascension, and the baptism of the Holy Spirit. We are living in an age of overlap. The age to come has broken into this age, but the old age continues along with it.

Then what is the gospel? It is the invitation to now live in and from the Kingdom of God. As Dallas Willard states in his book *The Divine Conspiracy*, the good news is that "the Kingdom of God is available to you." This is the meaning of "at hand."

Dispensationalism and the Kingdom of God

I want to return to the view of dispensationalism, which has been the major view of American evangelicals and Pentecostals since about 1925. The original Pentecostal movement was not dispensational, but it became so. Dispensationalism swept the Bible schools and churches from about 1900 to 1930. It was developed by J.N. Darby in England in the middle of the past century. Darby was an Anglican who reacted against Anglicanism. The teaching was popularized by C. I. Scofield, and a man named A. C. Gaebelein was a prominent early defender (1900).

In the view of dispensationalism, we are living in "a dispensing of," or a way of God's acting in the world. In the view of those who hold this tradition, when Jesus preached the Kingdom of God, He offered it to the Jewish people with all of its prophetic ramifications. If the Jewish people in the first century as a whole had accepted it, they would have seen all their prophetic hopes fulfilled. The Kingdom of God would have come. They refused it. Then Jesus began to change His teaching and to prepare His disciples for something that was unforeseen prophetically. He began to prepare His disciples for a "Parenthetical Church Age." It is said that the Last Days have to do with Israel, but because Israel said no to the Gospel, Israel was scattered. Then came the church age. It was not an afterthought to God, but it seems like an afterthought to us. So we have the church age instead of the Kingdom of God. We do not preach the Gospel of the Kingdom of God. We preach the Gospel of the grace of God. The Gospel of the Kingdom says, "Repent, for the Kingdom of God is at hand (meaning all of His judgments and the dawning of the age to come). The wolf is going to lie down with the lamb." That is the Gospel of the Kingdom.

The Gospel of the grace of God, in contrast, is said to be, "Receive Jesus as your Savior, be born again, and you will go to heaven." There is a distinction made in this theology between the Gospel of the grace of God and the Gospel of the Kingdom. It is said we do not teach the Gospel of the Kingdom; we preach the gospel of the grace of God. When the Church is raptured out of this world, before the Great Tribulation begins, then Elijah will reappear. The 144,000 will be on earth. While the Church is look-ing down from heaven at the scene on earth, 144,000 people of the nation of Israel will preach the Gospel of the Kingdom. It will be preached again because we will be at the stage, as in the first cen-tury, when the Kingdom can come in fullness.

There is a grain of truth in all this, maybe more than a grain. However, I have problems with the major thrust of the teaching. I want to share with you where I think the truth is and where I think the error lies.

The Kingdom Is Present in Healing, Signs, and Wonders

In classical dispensationalism, signs, wonders, and miracles are connected with preaching the Gospel of the Kingdom. The blind receiving their sight, the lame walking, the deaf hearing, demons being cast out, and the dead being raised up are signs of the Kingdom. Since the Kingdom has been postponed, what fol-lows in this teaching? The gifts of the Spirit are not for this "Par-enthetical Church Age," according to dispensationalist thought! It is interesting that Acts notes that Paul, who experienced signs, wonders, and miracles in his ministry, preached the Gospel of the Kingdom (chapter 28). You can only accept the dispensational view if you are selective in your use of texts.

The truth of this view is in the fact that the fullness of the Kingdom of God described in the prophets had not yet come. There is a certain postponement feeling to that. It is not because the Kingdom of God has not come. We are to preach the gospel of the Kingdom. Signs do follow.

Two Understandings of the Gospel

I want to give you an idea of what I believe is the difference between the dispensational gospel of the grace of God and the biblical Gospel. I do preach the Gospel of the grace of God. However, I preach it as part of a larger context. I preach the Gospel of the grace of God, but not in contrast to the Gospel of the Kingdom.

The dispensational gospel of the grace of God sounds like this: "John, do you know that you are going to heaven? You don't? Well, John, I want to tell you how you can go to heaven. Jesus died for your sins. If you receive Him into your heart, you will go to heaven." If John asks, "Will I have to live differently?" the answer is, "No, John, you do not have to live differently. If you had to live differently, salvation would not be obtained by grace. You can receive Jesus as Savior and not receive Him as Lord. However, you will not live a fulfilled life and really be happy if you continue to live in sin. If you want to live an unfulfilled life and still go to heaven, you can do it. At least receive Jesus and go to heaven."

Some dispensationalists might tell you that if a person cannot sin like a total pervert for the rest of his life after receiving Jesus and still go to heaven, then salvation is not by grace. Grace is not defined by God's favor, which gives us the power to change. Grace is defined as a forgiveness that one can receive without having to submit to Jesus as Lord. It is a tenet of classical dispensational theology that you can receive Jesus as Savior without receiving Him as Lord. It is taught; it is argued. You can read it for yourself in numerous journals and books. Dispensationalists even smell danger in the view that we must receive Jesus as Lord to be saved. (The reader can look up Zane Hodges' *Lordship Salvation*.) The reason I raise this issue is that the Church is so influenced by it and doesn't even know it.

This understanding is in great contrast to the true Gospel of grace, which I call the Gospel of the Kingdom. "John, your life is a mess, but Jesus came to turn your life around. If you are willing to respond to the Holy Spirit's conviction, you can receive grace, the gift of God, and come under the rule of Jesus. If you come under the rule of Jesus, everything in your life will change. Not only will you have everlasting life—if you were to die—but your life will be turned right side up here and now. The Kingdom of God includes His promises of deliverance, wholeness for your life, and material provision. If you walk with your heavenly Father, every dimension of your life can be changed. God offers you nothing less than a whole new life in every area through the death, resurrection, and ascension of Jesus. God's transforming power is offered to you whereby you can live according to His ways. Enter the Kingdom of God by receiving Jesus as Savior and Lord." That is the Gospel of the Kingdom.

I believe in the Gospel of the Kingdom. I believe that the Gospel we preach is the Gospel of the Kingdom. It is the same signs-and-wonders Gospel that was always intended. The postponement of the Kingdom of God is understood in the sense that it has only come partially and not in its fullness. This relates to the role of the Church in the age of transition. Yet the Kingdom was not postponed. It just needs to grow and develop in its manifestation until the age to come. We understand the present Kingdom manifestation as partial.

The Parables of the Kingdom of God
The Four Soils

The parables of the Kingdom of Heaven or of the Kingdom of God give us the same understanding of the Kingdom. The first is the parable of the four soils. We must understand what Jesus was teaching in this parable. He was describing how the Kingdom of God could come in reality and not in totality. He was describing how the Kingdom of God could be already, but not yet. The Kingdom of God has not been postponed, but the Kingdom of God in fullness has not yet come.

> *Then he told them many things in parables, saying: "A farmer went out to sow his seed. As he was scattering the seed, some fell along the path, and the birds came and ate it up. Some fell on rocky places, where it did not have much soil. It sprang up quickly, because the soil was shallow. But when the sun came up, the plants were scorched, and they withered because they had no root. Other seed fell among thorns, which grew up and choked the plants. Still other seed fell on good soil, where it produced a crop—a hundred, sixty or thirty times what was sown. He who has ears, let him hear." The disciples came to him and asked, "Why do you speak to the people in parables?" He replied, "The knowledge of the secrets of the kingdom of heaven has been given to you, but not to them."*   Matthew 13:3-11

"Mystery" in the New Testament describes something previously hidden that is now being revealed. The fact that the Kingdom of God could come in reality but not totality was previously hidden, but is now being revealed. Paul understood another mystery in this stage of the manifestation of the Kingdom: the Jew and Gentile can now be one in the Messiah. It is the revelation that God is creating the Bride of the Messiah in this transitional age to rule in the age to come. The Jewish people expected that there would be an age in which Jew and Gentile would be one, but not until Israel was delivered from her enemies and the Messiah was ruling and reigning. In the age to come, Jew and Gentile will be one. His name will be one in all the earth. The mystery that was given to Paul was that Jew and Gentile could be one now, in this stage of the Kingdom of God, before the fullness of the manifestation of the Kingdom. This is another example of the word *mystery*, previously hidden but now revealed.

> *Whoever has will be given more, and he will have an abundance. Whoever does not have, even what he has will be taken from him.*   Matthew 13:12

People who respond to revelation get more. People who are hardened to the revelation they have get less revelation.

> *Listen then to what the parable of the sower means: When anyone hears the message about the kingdom and does not understand it, the evil one comes and snatches away what was sown in his heart. This is the seed sown along the path. The one who received the seed that fell on rocky places is the man who hears the word and at once receives it with joy. But since he has no root, he lasts only a short time. When trouble or persecution comes because of the word, he quickly falls away. The one who received the seed that fell among the thorns is the man who hears the word, but the worries of this life and the deceitfulness of wealth choke it, making it unfruitful. But the one who received the seed that fell on good soil is the man who hears the word and understands it. He produces a crop, yielding a hundred, sixty or thirty times what was sown.*   Matthew 13:18-23

You can apply this principle to any promise of Scripture. It will be fruitful in your life if you hear it and receive it. The Word of God is the means of coming into faith to receive the promise of God. In this parable Yeshua taught that the manifestation of the Kingdom of God, in this transitional period, is a stage of seed sowing, a stage previously hidden but now revealed. It is a stage of seed sowing in which different soils will respond to the message of the Kingdom. There are three ways to respond improperly. These ways are represented by three soils or hearts. One is the hard heart that doesn't receive at all. The second is the heart that seems to receive excitedly, but only experiences a surface emotion. The third is the heart that seems to receive, but cares and riches choke out the Word. There are those who receive the message of the Kingdom of God with all of its promises. Their lives bring forth fruit—thirty, sixty, and a hundredfold. Their lives change and produce change in others. So we could say the Kingdom of God is coming and has come.

The Kingdom of God is present among us in this stage of seed sowing, and the Lord extends an offer to people to come into that Kingdom and be fruit bearers in the Kingdom. Three kinds of people will not come in; one kind will. The Kingdom of God will be manifested through those who receive the seed of the Gospel. Jesus is preparing His disciples for a period of seed sowing in which three kinds of people will reject it and one kind will accept fully.

The Parable of Wheat and Weeds

Jesus told them another parable: "The kingdom of heaven is like a man who sowed good seed in his field. But while everyone was sleeping, his enemy came and sowed weeds among the wheat, and went away. When the wheat sprouted and formed heads, then the weeds also appeared. The owner's servants came to him and said, 'Sir, didn't you sow good seed in your field? Where then did the weeds come from?' 'An enemy did this,' he replied. The servants asked him, 'Do you want us to go and pull them up?' 'No,' he answered, 'because while you are pulling the weeds, you may root up the wheat with them. Let both grow together until the harvest. At that time I will tell the harvesters: First collect the weeds and tie them in bundles to be burned; then gather the wheat and bring it into my barn.'"   Matthew 13:24-30

Another image in Isaiah depicts both a harvest of wrath and a harvest of salvation at the end of the age. When the Kingdom of God comes in fullness there will be a separation of the wheat and tares. In this age the Kingdom of God produces good seeds that sprout and grow side by side with bad plants sown by the Kingdom of satan. An evil society will continue alongside the Kingdom of God. Sometimes those tares will even show up in the midst of the people of God. The Kingdom is here, but the tares are close to our garden. At other times the Kingdom of God will vanquish the tares of the enemy in the progress of the Kingdom. The good and evil seed, the good and evil planter, and the good and evil society grow side by side until the end comes.

This is an important parable for those who believe that the Body of believers will take over the whole world and live in righteousness for a thousand years before Yeshua comes again. That concept is known as postmillennialism. It holds that Jesus will come after the Church has ruled for a millennial age of peace on earth. Some great men of God believed that, including D. L. Moody (in his early years), Charles Finney, and Jonathan Blanchard (the founder of Wheaton College). This parable is forceful evidence against their view.

The Parable of the Mustard Seed

He told them another parable: "The kingdom of heaven is like a mustard seed, which a man took and planted in his field. Though it is the smallest of all your seeds, yet when it grows, it is the largest of garden plants and becomes a tree, so that the birds of the air come and perch in its branches." Matthew 13: 31-32

The Kingdom of God will grow from a small beginning in Israel to become a worldwide tree of God's people. It will take time to grow. It will not come all at once as many were expecting. The age to come has broken in, and it will continue to break in more and more.

The Interpretation of Wheat and Weeds

He answered, "The one who sowed the good seed is the Son of Man. The field is the world, and the good seed stands for the sons of the kingdom. The weeds are the sons of the evil one, and the enemy who sows them is the devil. The harvest is the end of the age, and the harvesters are angels. As the weeds are pulled up and burned in the fire, so it will be at the end of the age. The Son of Man will send out his angels, and they will weed out of his kingdom everything that causes sin and all who do evil. They will throw them into the fiery furnace, where there will be weeping and gnashing of teeth. Then the righteous will shine like the sun in the kingdom of their Father. He who has ears, let him hear." Matthew 13:37-43

This parable puts forth a picture of the Kingdom of God as having broken into this age. It is growing and developing in the midst of a society that also has sons of the devil. The good and evil are growing in the midst of this world. The world is coming to a climax in which there will be a great harvest of good and evil. The end of this transitional age brings a climactic judgment that will lead to the Kingdom of God coming in fullness.

The Last of the Last Days

By "the last of the Last Days" I mean the time of the events leading up to the return of Jesus. I want to review what I believe are some of the pivotal passages on these Last Days. This will be the foundation for interpreting the rest. Let me introduce this by saying I believe it is a mistake of classical teaching on the Last Days, especially in dispensational circles, to begin with the Books of Revelation and Daniel and try to plot things out from there.

Dispensational Teaching

According to dispensational Bible teaching, Jesus could come at any minute because there is nothing prophetically that must occur before He comes again. This is so ingrained in the Church that it is hard for people to realize this is not the historic view of the Church. It is a relatively recent view that has gained prominence since 1840. The reason Jesus could come at any moment in this view is because the prophetic Scriptures are interpreted to refer to the last Tribulation period during which the Church is no longer here. It is the Rapture of the Church that initiates the very last of the Last Days. It is said that as this "Parenthetical Church Age" comes to an end, Jesus can come any minute. When He returns, believers will disappear.

According to this pre-Tribulation Rapture view, seven years before Jesus' actual return to earth, He will come in the clouds to receive His Church. We will go up with Him for seven years while the events of Revelation 4–19 occur on the earth. During that time Israel will be the center of God's focus. The Gospel of the Kingdom will be preached by the 144,000. Elijah and Enoch will return as the two witnesses of Revelation 11. The antichrist will make his pact with Israel for the first three and one-half years, then break it and cause the wrath of God to come. There will be a Tribulation temple where sacrifices will be offered again. At the end of that seven years the Church will return with Jesus, defeat the enemies of Israel, and establish the millennial age.

Although dispensational teachers say that the next event of eschatology is the Rapture, they believe there could be many signs of the times that reflect the beginnings of what will be seen in the Tribulation period. These signs do not necessarily need to take place prior to the Rapture. If you see these signs coming to pass, preparing for what will happen during the Tribulation, you will know you are getting close to the Rapture. I am not convinced that this teaching is scriptural.

The Teaching of Jesus on Events Before He Comes

Matthew records the perspective of Jesus:

> *O Jerusalem, Jerusalem, you who kill the prophets and stone those sent to you, how often I have longed to gather your children together, as a hen gathers her chicks under her wings, but you were not willing. Look, your house is left to you desolate. For I tell you, you will not see me again until you say, "Blessed is he who comes in the name of the Lord."* Matthew 23:37-39

Jesus was speaking here of the leadership in Jerusalem. It was not the people who rejected Him, but the leadership. The people followed their leaders. The house is the temple and the whole governmental system with its prominence and importance. The leadership had their status through the temple and through Jerusalem, the capital of Israel. This would all be ended.

It is common in the Last Days teaching to believe that Israel will turn and accept Jesus. This is correct according to Zechariah.

And I will pour out on the house of David and the inhabitants of Jerusalem a spirit of grace and supplication. They will look on me, the one they have pierced, and they will mourn for him as one mourns for an only child, and grieve bitterly for him as one grieves for a firstborn son.   Zechariah 12:10

I believe these passages imply that a recognized leadership among the Jewish people will make a confession toward Yeshua, even, "*Blessed is He who comes in the name of the Lord.*" Then they will mourn.

But he who stands firm to the end will be saved. And this gospel of the kingdom will be preached in the whole world as a testimony to all nations, and then the end will come.   Matthew 24:13-14

This indicates that the Gospel will be preached in all the world as a witness first. Jesus is not going to come back until the Gospel of the Kingdom is preached in all the world. How does the dispensationalist handle that? Remember, to the dispensationalist the Church does not preach the Gospel of the Kingdom. The Church will be gone! So it is the Jewish saints during the Tribulation who will preach the Gospel of the Kingdom throughout the world. His coming here does not refer to the Rapture. It refers to the time later when He actually comes to earth to establish His reign. However, we have dispensed with the dispensational distinction between the Gospel of the Kingdom and the Gospel of the grace of God. You now understand why this is so important for the Last Days. I believe what Jesus is saying is, "When the Gospel of the Kingdom has been adequately preached to all the people groups of the world with demonstrations of the power of the Spirit, then the end will come." The "end" here is the end of this age and the full dawning of the age to come. It is the end of this transitional age when the Kingdom of God is progressing and growing, where wheat and tares grow together. The end is the return of Jesus. The Gospel of the Kingdom will be preached in all the world as a witness, and then the end will come.

The Coming of Jesus

At that time the sign of the Son of Man will appear in the sky, and all the nations of the earth will mourn. They will see the Son of Man coming on the clouds of the sky, with power and great glory. And he will send his angels with a loud trumpet call, and they will gather his elect from the four winds, from one end of the heavens to the other.   Matthew 24:30-31

This passage speaks about the Rapture. It will come after the gospel of the Kingdom is preached all over the world as a witness (see 2 Pet. 3:12 as well).

Repentance Before He Returns

Repent, then, and turn to God, so that your sins may be wiped out, that times of refreshing may come from the Lord, and that he may send the Christ, who has been appointed for you—even Jesus. He must remain in heaven until the time comes for God to restore everything, as he promised long ago through his holy prophets.

Acts 3:19-21

Peter thought that the restoration of all things, that is the Kingdom coming in fullness, would occur after the Jewish people repented. So he said, "*Repent that God might send Jesus who will remain in heaven until the times of the restoration of all things.*" While the restoration of the Church is taking place and has been taking place since the Reformation, the restoration of all things comes after Jesus no longer remains in heaven. Peter believed one of the keys to the restoration of all things, the coming of Jesus, is Jewish repentance. Of course, the leadership saying *"Blessed is He who comes in the name of the Lord"* is something Peter had in mind. I believe the restoration of the Church includes restoration to its Jewish roots.

How the Disciples First Understood the Last Days

It is important to see how the disciples understood the Last Days. One of the things that puzzles Christians is why the disciples did not at first go out and preach the Gospel to the whole world. Why is it that when Peter preached to Cornelius, it was so controversial? Why did Peter have to have a vision of seafood dishes before he was willing to preach to Cornelius? Peter had the vision of the sheet filled with unclean animals three times (Acts 10). The usual Christian view is, "Oh, those proud Jews, they just did not understand that God loves the Gentiles too. They thought the Gospel was for Jews only, and the Gentiles could not be saved. That is why they did not take the Gospel to the Gentiles." But that is not what happened. They had an incomplete picture of the Last Days. In their incomplete picture, taking the Gospel to the Gentiles did not make sense.

Peter understood that when Israel accepts Jesus as a whole, or when the leadership turns and blesses Him "who comes in the name of the Lord," then Israel will be delivered from her enemies, and the whole world will come to the knowledge of God. Peter and the apostles read the Scriptures. They understood that Jesus would be a light to the Gentiles, that the whole world would worship him, and that every nation would send representatives to the feast of *Sukkot* (Zech. 14). The issue was how to get to that point. The disciples' understanding was that when Israel was saved, that point would come. If they had been asked, "Why don't we go preach the Gospel to the Gentiles?" the answer would have been, "Why would we want to do that? If we can only get a few million Jewish people saved the whole world will come to the knowledge of God. If we go to the Gentiles, it will take forever." They understood that the Gentiles would ultimately come. It was the purpose of Israel to bring them. When Jesus commanded them to preach the Gospel in all the world and disciple the nations, they put it into their scheme of Last Days thinking.

I am not just speculating. Many ancient Jewish writings deal with the Last Days and corroborate this view. The Jews thought that being witnesses in Jerusalem, Judea, Samaria, and all the earth first referred to Jewish people, who are scattered to the utmost parts of the earth. Jesus said, "Go…and disciple the nations." "Sure," they must have thought, "we will disciple the nations— after Israel repents and turns to the Lord and is delivered from her enemies." They put it in a sequence that made a Gentile mission, at the time, look foolish. That is why Peter had to have the vision three times. When he obeyed the vision and went to Caesarea to minister to the household of Cornelius, the Spirit of God fell upon them while he was preaching the gospel. They spoke in tongues. Peter must have thought, "They have already received the Spirit from heaven and have not yet been baptized. Get them into the water quickly!" When he went back to Jerusalem, the other disciples asked him, "Why did you go up to preach to the Gentiles?" Some of them might have thought, "Has he lost his mind?" Peter said, "Who was I that I could resist the Holy Spirit?"

The whole purpose of all this was not only to get Cornelius saved, but to prepare the disciples for the ministry of Paul and others who would follow him. The disciples' response to Peter's preaching was perhaps parallel to the response of Yeshua. It is as if they were saying, "We are only called to the lost sheep of the house of Israel." The other nations were to be saved, but the most useful thing to do first was to go only to the lost sheep of the house of Israel. The disciples carried on the traditions of Jesus. It was not pride or Jewish ethnocentricity but a matter of strategy.

Bringing the Gospel to the Gentiles

Jesus said that the Gospel of the Kingdom would be preached in all the world as a witness, and then the end would come. God had to get this revelation into the disciples, who still didn't quite understand. What did He do? He looked down and said, "Who will I choose to bring the Gospel to the Gentiles? Should I pick Peter? I must pick a zealous person, one who really wants to serve Me— someone who is, in My eyes, the likely candidate, but who in everyone else's eyes seems the most unlikely candidate. I will choose the most orthodox Jewish person I can find, one who is persecuting the believers. Mr. Super Orthodox will give the Gospel to the Gentiles."

Paul was the logical choice. He sat at the feet of Gamaliel, the leading Jewish thinker of the day. He added another piece to the puzzle. His understanding of the Last Days combined Matthew 23 and 24 in the most ingenious way. He agreed with Peter that when Israel repents God will send Jesus. However, Paul believed that the spiritual power to get Israel saved would require a world movement of people from all nations. This turns our thinking upside down. We think after the flesh and not after the Spirit.

Two Things Precede Israel's Salvation

My understanding of Paul leads me to believe that two key things must precede Israel's salvation. *There must be a saved remnant of Israel that is still a recognizable part of Israel.* The remnant is part of the rest of the Body of believers, not separatistic. Jew and Gentile are one in Yeshua. However, the saved remnant is not only part of the Body universal but is part of Israel. That saved remnant is a key to the future of the whole nation. The second key is that *there must be a mighty move of God in all the nations of the world.* This last great move of God in world revival will bring the Church to John 17 unity, which will precede world redemption. This will provide sufficient spiritual power and manifestation, through intercession and demonstration, to turn Israel to God. You now realize how the Church has missed it.

> *Again I ask: Did they stumble so as to fall beyond recovery? Not at all! Rather, because of their transgression, salvation has come to the Gentiles to make Israel envious. But if their transgression means riches for the world, and their loss means riches for the Gentiles, how much greater riches will their fullness bring! I am talking to you Gentiles. Inasmuch as I am the apostle to the Gentiles, I make much of my ministry in the hope that I may somehow arouse my own people to envy and save some of them. For if their rejection is the reconciliation of the world, what will their acceptance be but life from the dead?* Romans 11:11-15

In a real sense, if we live out what God is calling us to do, we can hasten the day of His coming. He will see to it that He has a Last Days people who do just that.

Paul shows us here that one of the key reasons for salvation coming to the Gentiles is to provoke Israel to jealous desire for their own Messiah and the Gospel. Until the Church sees that one of the reasons for world missions is to see Israel saved, they will not have the Pauline perspective.

Before continuing with the Last Days subject, I want to outline for you the classic views on the Millennium.

63

The Postmillennial View

The postmillennialist believes that when Yeshua died, rose again, and went to heaven, a transitional age began, and in that transitional age the Body of believers grows. The postmillennialists include Charles Finney, Jonathan Blanchard (the founder of Wheaton College), and, some believe, Jonathan Edwards. His writings on the subject are not clear. Some of the Puritan revivalists in the seventeenth century also held this view. The Body of believers will continue to grow until á certain climax occurs. That climax is not the return of Yeshua. Instead, the Body of believers conquers the whole world for the Gospel, and all the world acknowledges Yeshua. The Body of believers reign for one thousand years. At the end of that one thousand years the Rapture spoken of in First Thessalonians will take place.

> For the Lord himself will come down from heaven, with a loud command, with the voice of the archangel and with the trumpet call of God, and the dead in Christ will rise first. After that, we who are still alive and are left will be caught up together with them in the clouds to meet the Lord in the air. And so we will be with the Lord forever.
>
> 1 Thessalonians 4:16-17

Next, postmillennialists believe that a new heaven, new earth, and new Jerusalem will come down out of heaven. What does postmillennial mean? Postmillennial means that Yeshua returns after a one-thousand-year rule on earth by the Body of believers. The Body of believers literally conquers the whole world. The key book that argues this view is *An Eschatology of Victory* by J. Marcellus Kik. Another who holds this view is Larraine Boetner, author of a book titled *The Millennium*.

Some postmillennialists say that the one thousand years is a literal thousand years; some say a thousand is ten times ten times ten, a symbol of completeness. It is not literal. This view is gaining ground today. Many people consider this the primary view of the "Kingdom Now Movement." It is not. Only ten to twenty percent of those who identify with that movement hold this postmillennial view.

Some who espouse the postmillennial view have been accused of being humanists. This is a false accusation. They are people who believe that human beings are so empowered by the Holy Spirit that through His power the whole world will come to the knowledge of God. This will occur through the work of believers, without the actual return of Yeshua. At the end of this millennial age there will be a falling away, spoken of in Revelation 20. Satan will be loosed for a season. It is taught that satan is now bound by the spiritual life of the Body, but he will be loosed for a season and then Yeshua will return. After that will come the Great White Throne Judgment. Some Calvinists believe that it is predestined that we take over the world. This answers the problem of those who might reject the Gospel due to free will.

The theme of Wheaton College, which I attended, was "For Christ and His Kingdom." The meaning reflected founder Jonathan Blanchard's vision of a training school to prepare believers for taking over the world. Charles Finney founded Oberlin College with the same vision. This is an historic view. The major problem with the postmillennial view is the biblical picture of the end of this age, especially the disciples' view that they could be alive at the time of His return and still be a minority in the world.

The Amillennial View

The predominant Christian view throughout the ages, held alike by Catholics, Protestants, Lutherans, Reformed, and many of the original Baptists, was amillennialism. Amillennial means "no literal Millennium." Some people would rather call this view present-milliennialism. The present-millennialist believes that Yeshua ascended and poured out His Spirit. The church age then began.

The church age is the age of the offer of the Gospel to the whole world. At the end of this age of the Millennium, the church age, Yeshua will return. Then will follow the Rapture, the resurrection, the translation, and the final judgment. After that will be the new heavens, the new earth, and the new Jerusalem.

Some would say, "If the millennial age started with the out-pouring of the Holy Spirit at Shavuot, Pentecost, then why is the world in such a mess? I thought the Millennium was an age of peace and prosperity." The amillennialist has several things to say about this. The amillennialist is less literal in dealing with Old Testament prophecy than both the premillennialist and the post-millennialist. First of all, he will say that those images in the Scriptures (of the wolf lying down with the lamb, no one making war, and people living to a very old age, etc.) are symbolic of the new heavens and new earth. They are not to be taken literally as a more perfect continuation of earthly reality. Amillennialism usu-ally holds that the Israel of God is now the Body of believers, Jew and Gentile. Many amillennialists, not all, do not have a place for Israel in their scheme because they look at the true Israel as being the Body of believers, the Church. (This is true of many postmil-lennialists as well.)

They would view prophecies about the regathering of Israel as prophecies about the Church being gathered unto the Lord at the end of the age. Much is based on how one looks at Revela-tion 20. They say that the thousand years of Revelation 20 is a symbolic number having to do with one of two possibilities (and here amillennialists differ). Some say that the thousand years pertains to the reign of saints in heaven. It is the souls in heaven with Yeshua that are reigning in their present existence. Others say (especially the faith charismatic people that have adopted an amillennialist view) that today believers rule on earth in a spiritu-al rule. The realm in which we take the Gospel to the nations and influence governments is partial, but it is real spiritual reigning in life. These folks do not believe that the Kingdom will dawn in fullness before Yeshua comes. The fullness awaits the new heaven and new earth. Most of them agree that the Kingdom is "already but not yet." The fullness of the Kingdom awaits the return of Yeshua. When Yeshua returns, we won't have a Millennium on this earth as we know it. The new heavens, new earth, and new Jerusalem will come into being. The millennial age is symbolic of the fact that the believers reign in life through Jesus. We are to reign in life, and our reigning in life is the symbolic Millennium. These might say, "The reason it does not seem to fit is that you are taking it too literally."

This view has become significant in the charismatic movement. It is classical Reformed theology (Presbyterian or Reformed). Some people believe that Israel will be preserved and saved at the end of this age and then enter the new heavens and new earth with those from the nations who are saved. A minority of amillennialists teach that there is a continuing role and place for Israel. Richard Lovelace of Gordon-Conwell Seminary holds this view. Joe Rosenfarb of Beth Messiah in Virginia Beach, Virginia, holds this view. It is possible to fit Israel, to an extent, into all millennial schemes. Most amillennialists today and in past years, however, have not acknowledged the place of Israel.

The amillennialist view is very significant in the Kingdom Now Movement. Kingdom Now is not a denial of the future Kingdom but a call to live our kingdom principles now in all areas of life. As I said, the amillennial view has been the majority view in the history of both the Catholic and Protestant Churches.

One important book on the amillennial view, *Prophecy and the Church*, was written by the late Oswald Allis of Westminster Seminary, formerly of Princeton. His book is a powerful defense of the amillennial view.

The Historic/Premillennial View

The premillennial view was espoused by some of the early Church fathers. One of them was Iraneus in the second century. Some Puritans held it. As Church history moved into the fourth century, premillennialists were accused of holding a foolish literal "Judaic (Jewish) view" of the Last Days and were mocked for it. Basically the premillennial view says this: When Jesus ascended and poured out His Spirit, this transitional age began. Historic premillennialism was held by the famous seventeenth-century Lutheran teacher J.O. Bangel, as well as by J. Barton Payne at Wheaton College. It was also the view held by the late George Ladd of Fuller Seminary in California.

The historic remillennialists believe that when Yeshua ascended and poured out His Spirit, the Kingdom came. The historic premillennialists believe that the Kingdom is already, but also not yet; they believe that the Kingdom is in the midst of this world. At the end of this transitional age, Yeshua will return. This includes a rapture of living saints and the resurrection of the saints who have died. We will meet Him in the air. A brief complex of events will culminate in the return of Yeshua with His saints to set up a one-thousand-year rule on earth. Those Jews who were not born again until this period will be part of the nation of Israel on earth in a literal millennial age, a one-thousand-year age on earth. Both Israel and the nations will embrace Yeshua as King and Savior. Israel will be the capital of the nations in that age.

Satan will be bound during that thousand-year reign, and the conditions described in the prophets will come into being. In an earthly existence, people will fully live out the promises of God. At the end of that age, characterized by a spiritual backsliding, satan will be loosed. The amillennialists say satan is bound with regard to the authority of the Church today. The premillennialists say satan will be bound more literally and loosed at the end of the thousand years. Then will come the final judgment, the Great White Throne. After the Great White Throne Judgment, the new heavens and new earth will appear. Everybody agrees that someday we will get to the new heavens, the new earth, and the new Jerusalem. The thousand years is really the fulfillment of the prophetic hope. However, the one thousand years is still somewhat transitional, even though a very ideal age. This is historic premillennialism. This is where I am with some significant additions that we will explain in other chapters. I believe the Scriptures speak about an age in which the promises of faith will be attained on a worldwide scale.

Where will the Church be during this period? While Israel will be the capital of the nations, the Church is described as the ruling Bride by the side of the Messiah. So indeed the Church is made up of Jew and Gentile, but in that age it is those Jews and Gentiles who are in their transformed spiritual bodies who rule with Him.

Dispensational Premillennialism

This is a relatively recent position. Dispensational premillennialism has been the majority view of the American evangelical Church for the last seventy years. I am not in the majority. The dispensational premillennialist says that when Israel refused the kingship of Yeshua during His life, the Kingdom was postponed for a parenthetical church age. Israel was put on a shelf. God is now seeking to call out a people to be saved. At the end of this church age, the saints will meet the Lord in the air. They will stay in heaven with Him for a seven-year period during the Tribulation on earth. At that time God will begin to move through Israel, and 144,000 saved men will give a Kingdom witness. He will return with His saints (us) to put down the enemies of Israel and inaugurate the one-thousand-year literal rule. At the end of this will come the judgment, followed by the new heavens and new earth.

Some dispensational premillennialists look at the Millennium differently. They say it is an age when people are generally saved. Others say it is an age when the saints will rule over unsaved people, all of whom will rebel in the end. They will all go to hell except for the Jewish people. I have read both views. The Millennium is a matter of some disagreement.

Premillennial dispensationalists include people like John Walvord of Dallas Theological Seminary, Charles Ryrie of the *Ryrie Study Bible*, Dwight Pentecost of Dallas, the late Alva Mc-Clean, Charles Feinberg in California, and many others.

Both the charismatic and Pentecostal movements include those who hold these different viewpoints on the Last Days. The verbal war over these views is intense, but some do not really understand the viewpoint of the other. I do believe I understand because I was educated in the different views under leading proponents. May God forgive us for our lack of charity in how we deal with brothers and sisters who hold to different views on these issues. May we gain His heart. In the charismatic world and to a lesser extent in the messianic Jewish world, an ungodly war rages over these issues.

The Postmillennial/Amillennial Combination

Today a new view is gaining adherents. A combination of postmillennialism and amillennialism, this view believes the Church will take over the whole world. When it does, the thousand-year period will be complete. Then Yeshua will return and establish the new heavens and new earth.

I am an historic premillennialist. The case for this view and the purpose of the millennial age will be addressed in greater detail in Chapters 6 and 9. Until then, we will continue our presentation on the biblical picture of the last of the Last Days.

CHAPTER 3

RESTORATION OF THE CHURCH AND THE JEWISH REMNANT

by Daniel Juster

The Last Days and the Restored Church

In Romans 11, the Scripture puts forth a pattern for the Last Days. Not many people look at Romans as having to do with the Last Days, but these chapters are very important for our study. It is my belief that if you study these Scriptures in context, you will find that the return of Yeshua is in some way contingent, connected to, or dependent upon the people of God fulfilling their role. The Body of believers, Jew and Gentile, must give an adequate demonstration and witness to the Kingdom in all the nations of the world. Jewish leadership must also see a strong messianic Jewish movement in the midst of Israel and the Jewish community worldwide. This will prepare the leaders to reverse the decision of their first-century counterparts and say, "*Blessed is He who comes in the name of the Lord.*" You will find that the return of Jesus is not something that just happens "in the sweet by and by," as the old hymn goes. Yeshua will come; we will see Him in glory, but it will not just happen!

Peter said that we are to hasten the day of His coming (2 Pet. 3). He said to a Jewish audience, "*Repent that* [God] *might send Jesus.*" Jesus said, "*You will not see Me until you say, 'Blessed is He who comes in the name of the Lord.' *" Paul said, "*What will* *their acceptance be but life from the dead?*" In other words, establishing the saved remnant of Israel will lead to the whole of Israel being saved and will result in life from the dead.

> *Again I ask: Did they stumble so as to fall beyond recovery? Not at all! Rather, because of their transgression, salvation has come to the Gentiles to make Israel envious. But if their transgression means riches for the world, and their loss means riches for the Gentiles, how much greater riches will their fullness bring! I am talking to you Gentiles. Inasmuch as I am the apostle to the Gentiles, I make much of my ministry in the hope that I may somehow arouse my own people to envy and save some of them. For if their rejection is the reconciliation of the world, what will their acceptance be but life from the dead?* Romans 11:11-15

Verse 15 refers to the resurrection and return of Yeshua. Truly there is a dimension of life from the dead when Jewish people accept Yeshua. Somehow a spiritual battle is won in the heavenlies that leads to the pouring out of blessing upon all nations. However, I believe the language here, as in Romans 8, looks toward that ultimate climax of this age, despite these other good applications. Paul says there is a saved remnant that proves the continued validity of God's covenant love for Israel. The saved remnant needs to grow and become established so that it leads to all Israel being saved. This leads to the resurrection from the dead. By the same token, the Gospel of the Kingdom must be preached in all the world as a witness; then the end comes.

> *But he who stands firm to the end will be saved. And this gospel of the kingdom will be preached in the whole world as a testimony to all nations, and then the end will come.* Matthew 24:13-14

To fulfill this, there must be a restored people of God, Jew and Gentile. Born-again Jewish people are part of the Body of believers universal and the saved remnant of Israel. The restored Body of believers that is so empowered fulfills the role to which God has called us. This fulfills the charges of God that the Body of believers go into all the world and preach the Gospel to every creature, reflecting mercy and love to Israel.

John 17 and the Last Days

My prayer is not for them alone. I pray also for those who will believe in me through their message, that all of them may be one, Father, just as you are in me and I am in you. May they also be in us so that the world may believe that you have sent me. John 17:20-21

John 17 has not commonly been considered a passage of Last Days doctrine, or eschatology, but the great founder of modern missions, Ludwig Von Zinzendorf in Germany, considered it to be so. Here Yeshua prays for His disciples to come into unity, power, and oneness. In verse 20, He makes some amazing statements as He prays. I do not believe Yeshua ever prayed a prayer that could not be or would not be answered. If Jesus prayed this prayer, it will be answered. It may be that we need to lend prayer support to this prayer and be in unity and longing for the same thing.

In His prayer, Jesus is looking beyond His immediate disciples. God has given His glory to His people, but I would like to suggest that we don't always manifest that glory. He says that He has given us the glory of God that we might be one. I can't absolutely prove this from the text, but it is my belief that the glory Yeshua has given is the fullness of the Holy Spirit. We must enter into this. The indwelling glory and the manifest glory of God in us is His Spirit. The Spirit is given that we might manifest a unity or oneness like the oneness Yeshua has with the Father. Their hearts beat in unity. Their desires are one. They agree on everything.

A Prayer for Agreement and Glory

At our level, however, He is talking about a basic agreement on those things that are important, that we would be one as He and the Father are one, and that we would manifest His glory. We are to become a people like unto Yeshua who manifest the power and love of God. This is seen in preaching the Gospel of the Kingdom, healing the sick, raising the dead, cleansing the lepers, and casting out demons. If the glory is there, the manifestation of that glory in signs and wonders and greater works will also be there. That is why He said to His disciples, *"It is a good thing that I go away, because if I go away I will send the Comforter."* The Comforter enables us to enter into His glory, to do like works, to be a united people of God. To fully manifest this, we must come into unity in the Spirit and a basic understanding of God's values and teaching. He describes it in John 17.

> *I in them and you in me. May they be brought to com-*
> *plete unity to let the world know that you sent me and*
> *have loved them even as you have loved me.* John 17:23

I believe Yeshua is praying nothing less than the fulfillment of the prophets' hope. He is praying to the Father that the world might come to the knowledge of God. When He prays that the world might believe (many people think the world will never believe), He is not praying that the world might bend the knee before the last judgment and go to hell anyway. No, I believe He is praying for the fulfillment of the prophets' hope that the knowledge of the Lord will cover the earth as the waters cover the sea. If that is what He is praying for, then He is praying for believers to come to a place of manifesting glory because we are a key to the fulfillment of the prophetic hope.

74

Therefore, I believe it is necessary, before Jesus returns, for the Body of believers to come into this place and be part of the series of events that will lead the world to believe. The world will believe as a result of believers coming into the place for which Jesus prayed. That is astonishing for some people, but if you check it out I think you will find this is exactly what Scripture has in mind. I believe Ephesians 4:11-16 is speaking of the same thing. One of the keys to this unity is the restoration of the fivefold ministry and its equipping of the saints until we all come to the unity of faith.

That We Might Be With Him

Father, I want those you have given me to be with me where I am, and to see my glory, the glory you have given me because you loved me before the creation of the world.   John 17:24

Glory is "heaviness" in Hebrew, the bright shining glory and heaviness of God. Yeshua says, "I pray that they might be with Me where I am that they might behold My glory." I do not believe as many evangelicals do that Jesus was praying here for His followers to go to Heaven when they die. That would have been a strange thing to pray. All Jewish people who were faithful believed they would. Mary, when Lazarus died, said they would see Lazarus again in the resurrection. I believe Jesus was praying for the Body of believers to manifest His glory and unity, because when they did the complex of events would unfold that would lead the world to believe. This is connected to them being with Him where He is, being translated into glory. It means the veil is stripped away. It means we meet Him; we see Him face to face. This can happen partially in spiritual experiences and revivals. However, it happens fully to the whole Body in the resurrection and translation (Rapture).

We must review the sequence of events in the Last Days and see how this fulfillment comes about in terms of the restoration of the Body. Pentecost, I believe, was the high point for the Body. The 120 were gathered in unity and received the glory of the Spirit. The Last Days Body will go beyond what was experienced at Pentecost.

The Last Days Body, coming into that place worldwide, effects a completion of its witness, Israel's confession of Yeshua; then we will be with Him where He is. The return of Yeshua is connected to believers' fulfilling their role in history in this transitional age. It could happen rapidly.

Romans 8 and the Last Days

Keeping in mind what Jesus said in John 17, let us relate it to Romans 8. What did Jesus say? *"I have given them the glory...that they may be one...that the world might believe...and that they may be with me where I am."* That was the sequence.

> *I consider that our present sufferings are not worth comparing with the glory that will be revealed in us.*
>
> Romans 8:18

What glory? The fullness of the manifestation of the Spirit. Even more, I believe, He is talking about the glory that will be revealed in us when we are translated and resurrected to be with Him where He is. We will have glorified bodies like His. You might take "glory" as the beginning stage of that oneness, but ultimately the glory is to be revealed when we are caught up together with Him and see Him face to face.

> *The creation waits in eager expectation for the sons of God to be revealed. For the creation was subjected to frustration, not by its own choice, but by the will of the one who subjected it, in hope.*   Romans 8:19-20

76

In other words God, as a judgment, subjected the creation to a certain futility. Creation does not reflect the ideal God has in mind for it.

> *That the creation itself will be liberated from its bondage to decay and brought into the glorious freedom of the children of God. We know that the whole creation has been groaning as in the pains of childbirth right up to the present time. Not only so, but we ourselves, who have the firstfruits of the Spirit, groan inwardly as we wait eagerly for our adoption as sons, the redemption of our bodies. For in this hope we were saved. But hope that is seen is no hope at all. Who hopes for what he already has?*　　　　　　　　　　　　Romans 8:21-24

"Manifest Sons" Teaching

Paul believes that the manifestation of the sons of God in fullness will deliver the creation from its bondage to corruption (since the fall of Adam). A mistaken teaching (the "manifest sons" teaching) was put forth by some from the Latter Rain Movement. It was held that believers would come to such a place of glory before Jesus returns that many would walk around in resurrection bodies and be a genuinely supernatural people.

If you can see the error of this, perhaps you can also see the truth in it. Yes, the manifestation of the sons of God is what the creation is waiting for. It is a manifestation that takes place when we are joined together with Yeshua in the Rapture at the end of the age. Then we are manifested with Him. The Lord will come with ten thousands of His saints (Jude 14 and Zech. 14:5). The biblical writers in the new covenant were informed by these kinds of passages in the Hebrew Scriptures. However, there is an opposite error. If we are not to be manifest sons of God on this side of the resurrection, if we are not to go about in resurrection bodies, then are we to just wait till Jesus comes for all this to happen? No, this is also wrong!

A Correct Understanding of Manifest Sons

There is a dimension of coming into that place of unity and manifestation Yeshua prayed for on this side of the resurrection that is a necessary step to lead to the Rapture and the translation. *"That they might be one...that they might be with me where I am."* This is the manifestation of the sons of God. *"That they might be one"*—in the glory which He has given us on this side of the resurrection. Jesus said He has given the glory (John 17:22)!

So what is Paul saying? He is saying we groan within ourselves. It is like the birth pains of the Messiah of which the rabbis speak. Not only the creation, but we also who have the firstfruit of the Spirit groan within ourselves, eagerly awaiting the adoption, or the redemption of the body. Some people say this refers to the fact that people are getting sick and dying in pain; they are groaning, waiting for the resurrection of the body because their body is in physical pain and suffering. This is a very common view in evangelicalism, but that is not what Paul is saying here.

I believe he is talking about intercessory prayer, the groaning and travailing of the people of God. Intercessory prayer leads us into that place Jesus prayed for in John 17! This leads us into the time when Yeshua comes, to the full manifestation of the sons of God. We are participating in an intercessory groaning to lead up to that place of full manifestation of the sons of God, when we come with Him in glory. We are part of an intercessory groaning for the redemption of creation. We participate in that groaning that we might be translated or resurrected. Intercessory prayer of this kind is praying for the Body of Christ to fulfill its destiny.

The Last Days and Romans 9–11

Because Israel's destiny is bound to the destiny of the whole world, Israel's fulfilling her national destiny is connected to world redemption. However, the Church's fulfilling her destiny as a people, both Jew and Gentile, is also connected to world redemption and is a key to Israel's fulfilling her role! Paul, in Romans 9, is faced with a very difficult question. How is it that Jesus could be the Messiah and Israel could reject Him? How could that be just?

God Determines National Destinies

Paul's immediate response is to verbally slap the arrogant questioner. God is the one who chooses nations and kingdoms to play various roles of significance and insignificance throughout history. He talks about, *"Jacob have I chosen, and Esau have I hated."* This does not refer only to individuals but to the nations of Edom and Israel. Edom was the symbol of the evil nation in the Hebrew Scriptures. He first slaps the arrogant questioner, but then he goes on and gives a lesson in pottery to show that it is not just a brute choice on God's part.

> *Does not the potter have the right to make out of the same lump of clay some pottery for noble purposes and some for common use? What if God, choosing to show his wrath and make his power known, bore with great patience the objects of his wrath—prepared for destruction? What if he did this to make the riches of his glory known to the objects of his mercy, whom he prepared in advance for glory?* Romans 9:21-23

If you don't understand Middle Eastern pottery making you will not fully grasp what he is talking about here. When a potter made a vessel, if that vessel cracked, he would repair it. He would put wet clay on it, reheat it, and then refire it. If it held the patch, it was called a vessel of mercy. The potter would seek to repair the vessel several times; but if it would not hold his patch, it would become a vessel of wrath. He would finally break it and use the pieces for some other purpose.

Contrary to a harsh Calvinist interpretation of Romans 9, Paul is saying two things. First, it is up to the Potter to decide whether a nation is used for glory or for common purposes. God has His reasons; it is not arbitrary. Then he goes on to say that God bore with longsuffering the vessels that are fit for wrath. Bearing with longsuffering means that God sought to repair and put new wet clay on Israel several times; He sought to refine them and make them vessels of mercy. However, they did not hold their patch. They became vessels of wrath.

This is contrary to the belief that God predestined certain people to go to hell and predestined others for salvation. In chapter 10, he explains what happened to Israel and why they were not able, at that time, to be the nation of God's desire. (They did not hold the mercy patch that God sought to apply to them, but they would ultimately hold that mercy patch.) Why did Israel fail?

Brothers, my heart's desire and prayer to God for the Israelites is that they may be saved.   Romans 10:1

Why Israel Failed

Since they did not know the righteousness that comes from God and sought to establish their own, they did not submit to God's righteousness. Christ is the end of the law so that there may be righteousness for everyone who believes.   Romans 10:3-4

This passage, I believe, describes not only Israel in ancient times but the entire rabbinic Jewish orientation. Here God has given us the reason for Israel not entering in. The fault is not to be found primarily in God, but in Israel's response to God. Instead of being the vessels of mercy, they cracked and became brittle because they were seeking to establish their own righteousness. That is not the end of the matter.

Israel Is Not Ultimately Rejected

I ask then: Did God reject his people? By no means! I am an Israelite myself, a descendant of Abraham, from the tribe of Benjamin. Romans 11:1

If this means, as some amillennialists teach, that Jewish people can be saved like any other, what point is Paul making? Paul is saying the fact that some Jewish people are saved shows that there is still legitimacy to the nation as a whole. The fact there are true believers or true Christians filled with the Spirit proves the legitimacy of the institutional church, even though there has been much error. The saved remnant gives legitimacy to the whole.

God did not reject his people, whom he foreknew. Don't you know what the Scripture says in the passage about Elijah—how he appealed to God against Israel: "Lord, they have killed your prophets and torn down your altars; I am the only one left, and they are trying to kill me"? And what was God's answer to him? "I have reserved for myself seven thousand who have not bowed the knee to Baal." Romans 11:2-4

So Paul's answer to the unbelief of Israel is to point to the hope that comes out of the remnant that does believe. The remnant of Israel, if the argument is to make sense, is still recognizable as part of Israel. It is still a part of the Jewish nation.

So too, at the present time there is a remnant chosen by grace. And if by grace, then it is no longer by works; if it were, grace would no longer be grace. What then?

81

What Israel sought so earnestly it did not obtain, but the elect did. The others were hardened, as it is written: "God gave them a spirit of stupor, eyes so that they could not see and ears so that they could not hear, to this very day." And David says: "May their table become a snare and a trap, a stumbling block and a retribution for them. May their eyes be darkened so they cannot see, and their backs be bent forever."   Romans 11:5-10

Is Israel as a nation to forever have only a remnant that believes, with the nation as a whole remaining in unbelief? That is the next question.

Again I ask: Did they stumble so as to fall beyond recovery? Not at all. Rather, because of their transgression, salvation has come to the Gentiles to make Israel envious. But if their transgression means riches for the world, and their loss means riches for the Gentiles, how much greater riches will their fullness bring! I am talking to you Gentiles. Inasmuch as I am the apostle to the Gentiles, I make much of my ministry.   Romans 11:11-13

Paul asks, "Have they stumbled beyond recovery?" "Certainly not," is the answer. He is developing the idea that the salvation of Israel as a whole is a Last Days event. That salvation is connected to the fact that Israel as a whole needs to have a witness from the believing Gentiles. The saved among the Gentiles become a key to Israel's salvation.

The Responsibility of Gentile Believers

Paul uses his own life as an example for the Gentile believers corporately.

I make much of my ministry in the hope that I may somehow arouse my own people to envy and save some of them.
            Romans 11:13b-14

Magnifying the ministry means magnifying the work of the Holy Spirit. The ministry of believers is the work of the Holy Spirit. It is not magnifying self or ego. You must have the Holy Spirit doing mighty things or there is nothing to magnify. Secondly, you must publicize it through word of mouth, through newspapers, through radio and television, etc. "Magnify" means "publicize in a large way." Paul is telling us to follow his example.

Establish the Saved Remnant of Israel

This magnification will save some of Israel, a significant remnant. The purpose for getting that remnant saved is that it might lead to Israel's full acceptance. This in turn leads to the resurrection from the dead. If Jesus prayed in John 17 *"that they might be one that the world might believe,"* and if Paul talked about *"groaning and travailing for the manifestation of the sons of God,"* what kind of people do you suppose will constitute the Body of believers at the end of the age?

It will be a restored Body, a Bride that is made ready for the Messiah. This is seen in Ephesians 4:13,15 and 5:27. That is the quality of people required to fulfill this commandment of Paul to magnify the ministry, that we might see the saved remnant established. It will lead to life from the dead and the age to come.

Last Days Critical Mass

In addition to the Body of believers being restored, establishing the saved remnant of Israel, there will also be Last Days invasions, wars, and persecutions. This brings us to a point where this transitional age reaches critical mass. In a nuclear explosion, the "critical mass" is that point where the bomb needs only to be jarred by a trigger in just the right way to set it off. I believe this age will reach the critical mass point of world history. All the conditions will be right in the Body and the saved remnant of Israel.

The opposition to Yeshua and to the people of God is part of this critical mass according to the prophets.

Judgment and salvation will be ready to explode on the earth like a nuclear bomb. Only one element is necessary to push that critical mass to the point of explosion. That one thing is the confession of Israel's leadership, "*Blessed is He who comes in the name of the Lord.*" It will be the last thing that pushes this age of transition from critical mass into the spiritual explosion that leads to the age to come. It is the trigger.

I don't believe in a gradual taking over of the world until we rule everything. I do believe we play a part in the culmination of this age—along with the return of Yeshua.

The General Progression of the Last Days

Romans teaches that the magnification of ministry is something only a believing group can do. The book was written primarily to Gentiles. A believing group with the gifts and power of the Spirit has something to magnify before a watching world. That quality of spiritual life will manifest in such a way that it will make Jewish people jealous. This leads to a saved remnant from Israel (Rom. 11:14). That saved remnant from Israel, along with the saved Gentiles, will manifest the Kingdom of God in the John 17 fulfillment of Yeshua's prayer for unity. The Gentile believers with the saved remnant of Israel influence Israel's leaders to confess, "Blessed is He who comes in the name of the Lord." This leads to Israel's acceptance and life from the dead! Life from the dead implies the establishing of the age to come in fullness. The wolf will lie down with the lamb. The knowledge of the Lord will cover the earth as the waters cover the sea.

All Israel Will Be Saved

Romans again speaks about that pattern.

If the firstfruit is holy, the lump is also holy.

Romans 11:6 NKJV

What does that mean? It means that the lump, or unbelieving Israel, is holy because of the firstfruit of Israel that believes (the remnant).

If the root is holy so are the branches. Paul anticipates people saying, "Yes, but the branches were broken off in unbelief." If one does not ultimately believe in Yeshua, one is not saved and will not enter into Heaven or the Kingdom of God.

And if they do not persist in unbelief, they will be graft-ed in, for God is able to graft them in again.

Romans 11:23

This is just an *if*. It does not tell us whether it will happen or not. Paul later tells us.

After all, if you were cut out of an olive tree that is wild by nature, and contrary to nature were grafted into a cultivated olive tree, how much more readily will these, the natural branches, be grafted into their own olive tree!

Romans 11:24

The master Potter can repair even a vessel of wrath! The wild olive tree is the olive tree of the Gentile unbelievers. The fact that the olive tree of the people of God is called, with regards to Israel, their own olive tree should forever change theology for people who don't see the place of Israel. There is one olive tree with natural branches and formerly wild branches that have been grafted in. With regards to Israel, does this mean they will be grafted in? It is not yet clear. First, Paul says if they don't continue in unbelief, they will be grafted into their own olive tree. Then he makes it clear. They will be grafted back in! The logic is inescapable. However, some people try to escape the inescapable. Some say

85

that all Israel being saved means that all people, Jew and Gentile, who are born again will be saved. This is not what is means. The logic leads to the conclusion that the nation as a whole comes to Yeshua! (Among today's best exegetical scholars, this is almost universally seen.) The branches are preserved to be grafted back in.

I do not want you to be ignorant of this mystery, brothers, so that you may not be conceited: Israel has experienced a hardening in part until the full number of the Gentiles has come in. Romans 11:25

I believe that "the fullness of the Gentiles" means the full number of Gentiles will come in. The Kingdom witness that Jesus commanded in Matthew 24:13-14 will be fulfilled. The Gospel of the Kingdom will be preached in all the world as a witness, then the end will come. That brings in the full number of Gentiles as representatives from their nations. I also believe that "the fullness of the Gentiles," which is the understanding of the Greek, implies that the saved Gentiles will come into the fullness of power and glory that Jesus prayed for in John 17. Then Israel will come to Yeshua.

And so all Israel will be saved, as it is written: "The deliverer will come from Zion; he will turn godlessness away from Jacob. And this is my covenant with them when I take away their sins."

Israel Is Still Elect

As far as the gospel is concerned, they are enemies on your account; but as far as election is concerned, they are loved on account of the patriarchs, for God's gifts and his call are irrevocable. Romans 11:26-29

Israel is elect; they have a role; they have a gift; they have a calling—even world redemption. Their part in effecting world redemption is irrevocable. This is an amazingly clear verse, yet it is often ignored by those who teach that the Church fully replaced Israel.

> *Just as you who were at one time disobedient to God have now received mercy as a result of their disobedience, so they too have now become disobedient in order that they too may now receive mercy as a result of God's mercy to you.*　　　　Romans 11:30-31

I believe that whenever a Gentile brings a Jewish person to the mercy and love of God, we see an application of this. I believe, however, that he is talking about the whole nation receiving the mercy of God through the witness, prayer, and giving of the restored Body of believers.

All the World Shall Be Saved

> *For God has bound all men over to disobedience so that he may have mercy on them all.*　　　　Romans 11:32

Jews and Gentiles corporately are in view here. Now put it together that the knowledge of the Lord shall cover the earth as the waters cover the sea; that they might be one that the world might believe—it is the same promise! From Isaiah, to John 17, to Romans 8, to Romans 11, the same vision is in mind. The whole world comes to the knowledge of God. Paul sees the plan of God in terms of the Gentiles' salvation rebounding back upon Israel for her salvation, her reengrafting, which leads to the resurrection of the dead, which leads to the nations coming to the knowledge of God. He sees the whole sweep of the plan of God as we have been sharing it. That is why he loses himself in worship and acclamation and says:

> *Oh, the depth of the riches of the wisdom and knowledge of God! How unsearchable his judgments, and his*

paths beyond tracing out! Who has known the mind of the Lord? Or who has been his counselor? Who has ever given to God, that God should repay him? For from him and through him and to him are all things. To him be the glory forever! Amen.　　　　　　　　Romans 11:33-36

In the light of God's vast plan, Paul ends up worshiping, because when you see it, it brings you to your knees! The implication here is that if all Israel is saved, all the world will be saved too. At the end, after the judgments, Israel as a nation comes to God; the remaining nations come to God!

The Role of the Church

In Ephesians and other passages Paul talks about himself. He has been given a ministry and a revelation that was previously hidden. Jew and Gentile can now be one in the Messiah. What is the role of the Church? Remember, we said that in the Last Days view of the disciples in Jerusalem, after Israel was saved, she would be delivered from her enemies. Then the world would come to the knowledge of God. The mission to the nations, to different groups and peoples, included the mystery that Jew and Gentile would be one in the Messiah in this age. Certainly all the prophets taught that Jew and Gentile would be one in the Messiah in the millennial age. The mystery that was revealed to Paul is that they would be one and enter into salvation in this transitional age. In Acts 11 the disciples responded to Peter, "Well, what do you know, God has granted salvation even to the Gentiles, in this age, before we have been delivered, before all Israel has accepted it."

In addition Paul said that the Church is the Bride of the Messiah, that we rule with Him. Why, if God is going to save the nations after Israel is delivered, does He have this Gentile mission? Why are we seeking out all these people? There are several reasons for a world mission to the Gentiles and why Jew and Gentile will be one in the Body of believers. It would seem that this is a diversion. Why wasn't Peter's original perspective correct: that we would get Israel saved and then the nations would come? Why is it necessary to get all these Gentiles saved in this transitional age?

First, as Paul came to understand, the stubbornness and conflicts within Israel itself over Jesus and His death and resurrection make it necessary. Only a massive movement of spiritual power and prayer among the Gentiles will turn Israel to God. In Romans 11 he said, *"To make Israel jealous, salvation has come to the Gentiles."* One of the reasons for the witness to the Gentiles is to get Israel saved!

Second, if there is not a Gentile world mission, those people who die without Jesus will be lost. God wants people to enter into His kingdom and be saved!

The third reason, however, is the principle of representation, intercessory representation. God does not only weigh things individually; He weighs things corporately. I stand before you today in messianic Jewish ministry out of a heritage of believers on my mother's side who loved Israel, and out of my father's side as a Jew. There is a corporate "chosenness" in my family line. Every person who walks with God has a chosenness in his family line. If one walks with God as Abraham did, he has a similar chosenness. People, through intercession, bring God's chosenness to others.

Intercession is one of the ways that God has the legal grounds to enter into the situation. Some think it is unfair that everybody does not have the same chance. They have the humanistic ideal of the French revolution: liberty, equality, and fraternity. Margaret Thatcher once said she did not agree with the two hundredth anniversary celebration of the French Revolution. She did not think it was a revolution to celebrate. I agree with her. It was fully humanistic.

God judges the individual, but He also takes into account corporate realities. Moses intercedes for Israel, and Israel is not destroyed. Moses' righteousness and intercession are added into the equation, and Israel is saved. A mother intercedes and pleads for her children. More grace comes toward those children, and they are saved. I am not saying that intercession destroys free will, that it ultimately forces a person into the Kingdom against their will. However, it does bring the work of the Holy Spirit into the lives of those prayed for. One of the reasons for seeing people saved out of all the nations is that those people are being made part of the restored Bride. People from every nation, tribe, and tongue must play an intercessory role for the salvation of their nations and the salvation of Israel!

Israel is called a kingdom of priests. Priests are people who bring God and man together. It is a mediator role. Israel is a nation of priests. So Israel brings God to the nations and the nations to God. That is Israel's role as a nation. The Church is only metaphorically a nation because it is made up of people drawn from all nations.

The people drawn from all nations have the power to pray Israel into the place of saying, *"Blessed is He who comes in the name of the Lord,"* a prayer that welcomes Jesus to rule the world. Israel is a representative of the nations and therefore has the right to invite Jesus to rule the world. However, if Israel does not invite Jesus to rule the world, He won't. At the same time, Israel alone is not an adequate representation. There must also be representatives from each nation.

The representatives of each nation play an intercessory role. Just before Jesus comes, as I see it, the believers from every nation will be saying, in their various tongues, "Yeshua, maranatha! Come and rule over our nations." The Russian believers will say, "Lord Yeshua, come rule over Russia." The Japanese believers will say, "Lord Yeshua, come rule over Japan!" When that intercessory bank of prayer is filled to its completion from every nation, and Israel joins in prayer, world redemption will come! Of course, redemption comes with judgment. In judgment, wrath is poured out. God judges the world and then saves the world. If you understand this principle, you understand the meaning of being the Bride of the Messiah.

Israel and the Nations Repent

Zechariah 12:10 and 13 say that all Israel will mourn. *"They will look upon Him whom they have pierced and mourn for Him."* Matthew 24 states, however, that when they see the son of man, *"All the nations will mourn."* This is a worldwide *Yom Kippur* (Day of Atonement), a worldwide repentance. Those who foresee it pray that repentance into being so that the promise of the prophets will become reality. They will become Yeshua's Bride in fullness and have the privilege of ruling with Him from a resurrected state. The others come to the knowledge of God and form the millennial people of God. It is glorious to be the Bride, the resurrected rulers with Him during that age. This is why there is a mission to all the Gentiles, so that Yeshua will have a Queen to rule with Him in the messianic age, a Queen made up of the peoples from all nations. After the marriage supper of the Lamb, the Bride will take her throne as Queen!

Amos said that David's tent would be established and the Gentiles would flow to it (Amos 9). The Church of both Jew and Gentile in this age is a precursor and a foreshadowing of the millennial age, when Jew and Gentile worldwide will come to the knowledge of God. James' quote of Amos 9 in Acts 15 is a new application of the principle he saw there.

The Bride Comes With Jesus

In Thessalonica some people had died. What would their destiny be? And how would those living be reunited with them? Would they be the ones to complete the worldwide witness, to see the Body come into its fullness, and to see Jesus return? Paul thought he would see it all in his lifetime. They did not know. However, people were dying before Yeshua returned. They had not yet come into the fullness. Paul said to the Thessalonians:

> *Brothers, we do not want you to be ignorant about those who fall asleep, or to grieve like the rest of men, who have no hope. We believe that Jesus died and rose again and so we believe that God will bring with Jesus those who have fallen asleep in him.* 1 Thessalonians 4:13-14

This picture is so much a part of the New Covenant community that we have to recognize what a revolutionary thing it is. This truth has its foundation in the prophets.

> *According to the Lord's own word, we tell you that we who are still alive, who are left till the coming of the Lord, will certainly not precede those who have fallen asleep.* 1 Thessalonians 4:15

Why did he say that?—because he knew the Thessalonians were concerned for their loved ones.

> *For the Lord himself will come down from heaven, with a loud command, with the voice of the archangel and with the trumpet call of God, and the dead in* [Messiah] *will rise first.* 1 Thessalonians 4:16

I want to point out some things that are not usually seen here. If we believe that Jesus died and rose again according to verse 14, even so God is going to bring with Him those who are asleep in Jesus. In other words, when Jesus returns to this earth, He will return with His saints. Those who have died will be resurrected, and those who have been translated into their resurrected state, who were alive at the time of His coming, will return with Him. We are not to meet the Lord in the air and strum on harps in the clouds for eternity. We will be busy, for we are returning to rule with Him.

Before the whole world comes to the knowledge of God, the judgments will be devastating. The wrath of God will be great. In Zechariah 14 the prophet talks about the coming of Yeshua. He says that the Lord goes forth and fights, and we go forth with Him.

> *Then the LORD my God will come, and all the holy ones with him.* Zechariah 14:5b

That is what First Thessalonians is talking about when it says the Lord shall come with His saints. In other words, we are not raptured to sit up on the clouds but to be joined with Him and to come back with Him to rule and reign. What a wild experience that will be!

> *...God will bring with Jesus those who have fallen asleep in him.* 1 Thessalonians 4:14

The same is seen in the Book of Revelation. The image of the Rapture is that the Lord comes with His saints. Then we see them reigning with Him.

> *Blessed and holy are those who have part in the first resurrection. The second death has no power over them, but they will be priests of God and of Christ and will reign with him for a thousand years.* Revelation 20:6

I believe this is speaking about us. The same truth is found in Second Peter and Jude. The Lord is coming with His saints.

When Does Jesus Come?

Many people say, concerning the Rapture, that no one has any idea when it will take place. Yeshua did teach that no one knows the day or the hour, but He also taught us to discern the times and the seasons. It seems contradictory, but it really is not. God says that He does not do anything without revealing it to His servants, the prophets. There are prophets being restored to the Body of believers who are mightier than the ones who came before. Look around. God has begun to restore His prophets.

The idea of the Lord coming as a thief in Luke 17, as in the days of Noah, has to do with the fact that He comes unexpectedly to those who are in darkness. They are marrying and giving in marriage. They are living as they always have. They will be surprised by His coming. The passage on the Rapture in First Thessalonians helps us here. There were no chapter divisions when it was written.

> *Now, brothers, about times and dates we do not need to write to you, for you know very well that the day of the Lord will come like a thief in the night. While people are saying, "Peace and safety," destruction will come on them suddenly, as labor pains on a pregnant woman, and they will not escape. But you, brothers, are not in darkness so that this day should surprise you like a thief.*
>
> 1 Thessalonians 5:1-4

We will have a sense of when the Lord's return will happen. I believe that when the time is near, we will not know the exact day, hour, or moment, but we will know that it is near. We will be on our knees praying for the ultimate salvation of the world and Israel. This is the intercessory position I have described.

The Rebellion and the Anti-Messiah

Concerning the coming of our Lord Jesus [Messiah] and our being gathered to him, we ask you, brothers, not to become easily unsettled or alarmed by some prophecy,

94

report or letter supposed to have come from us, saying that the day of the Lord has already come. Don't let anyone deceive you in any way, for that day will not come until the rebellion occurs and the man of lawlessness is revealed, the man doomed to destruction. He will oppose and will exalt himself over everything that is called God or is worshiped, so that he sets himself up in God's temple, proclaiming himself to be God.

2 Thessalonians 2:1-4

Some thought that day would come quickly. They believed, like Thomas Munser during the Reformation, that they should drop everything and go up to a mountain and wait for the Lord. They left their work. Let me give a strong warning about people who say we are not to build, that we are to go to Israel, that the Last Days are upon us. That is exactly what happened to the Thessalonians. They started leaving their jobs. Yet, until the credible prophets of God confirm to us that the time has come, we are not to stop everything else.

God is establishing prophets in the earth. We will follow them when they speak. If they say, "Sell your building," "God wants you to leave," or "Don't leave," we will confirm such words in our spirits by His Spirit and will obey. God will have prophets with that credibility. However, in the New Covenant, each believer still must confirm the prophetic word in his spirit through the Holy Spirit. Until then, the Lord enjoins us to be ready for His soon coming and to maintain adequate oil in our lamps—should He delay (see Matt. 25:1-13).

Some people have developed an indifferent attitude about maintaining oil in their lamps and may be left high and dry. That was the problem of the Thessalonians. They were not putting oil in their lamps for the delay. In light of that, Paul gave some very important teachings. It is amazing to read and know that some dispensationalists derive the exact opposite meaning.

> *Don't let anyone deceive you in any way, for that day*
> *will not come until the rebellion occurs and the man of*
> *lawlessness is revealed, the man doomed to destruction.*
>
> 2 Thessalonians 2:3

This is an extremely controversial passage. It is used to support differing views of the Tribulation and Rapture. In context, I believe the passage indicates that the Rapture of which Paul spoke in First Thessalonians 4:16-17 comes after the antichrist is revealed. He is saying to not be troubled, as if the Rapture had already occurred. George Ladd, Robert Gundry, and others have demonstrated that he is clearly saying that we who are alive at His coming will have the antichrist before we see Jesus face to face. That day will not come until the son of perdition, or the man of sin, is revealed. This is quite contrary to the theory of the Rapture in the popular "Left Behind" series of novels.

There will come a time on earth when lawlessness will be given its full reign. The Body of believers will be present to witness that. Right now lawlessness is restrained. What restrains it is hotly debated. The pre-Tribulationists say the Holy Spirit in the Church restrains it. When the Church is taken out, the Holy Spirit is taken out. Then the antichrist can run wild with lawlessness. Others say that the restrainer is the providence of God in human government. God will remove that restraint. I lean toward the latter view. The dispensational pre-Tribulation view teaches that Paul is saying, "Don't be troubled as if the Lord had already come, for if the Lord had come and you missed it, you would now be seeing the antichrist." That is really not the natural sense of the text. He is saying that the antichrist will be revealed before the Rapture. Then we will all know that the time is nearing. We will be encouraged to "tough it through" for just a few more years. Then we will win. Another interpretation that has some credibility is that the restrainer is satan, that he is resisting the full victory of the Gospel and will do so until he is taken out of the way.

Protection for Believers

For the Body of believers it will be as it was for Israel in Goshen before the Exodus from Egypt. There will be martyrdom, but there will also be a Goshen. The Kingdom is present, and can make an impact on every area of life for the Gospel. We must do it. Contrary to the postmillennial view, however, ultimately there will be a deep contrast between the believing and unbelieving communities. Just before the Lord's return we will experience the greatest time of spiritual warfare.

Superficial Religion Blinds People and Leads to Sin

When I was growing up in the 1950s everybody went to church although most of them had a superficial religion. It was very difficult to witness to people who were not believers. They believed in living a good life. Young women believed in not sleeping around and not getting pregnant. Basically everybody believed in waiting until marriage. Everybody was "good." To tell people they had sinned and come short of the glory of God—they looked at their self-righteousness and didn't think they needed the Gospel. The liberal religion of the National Council of Churches flourished. God would rather us be hot or cold. That confusion, where unbelievers lived "good" lives in self-righteousness and pride, impeded the Gospel. It was humanism with Christian words, but with a different meaning.

And what happened? The unbelieving world decided to cast off all moral restraint because they did not believe the Gospel. Why not cast off moral restraint if you do not believe in the Gospel or that God gave the Law? In the last thirty years we have had dramatic change! Talk about ancient Israel turning from God!

When we came out of World War II victoriously, everyone was proclaiming God and country. We were for American values. By 1970, we were for sleeping around, for having children out of wedlock, and for abortion. The plagues have come and will be coming. The AIDS plague is going to get a lot worse. The lifestyle of the unbeliever is going to be a total contrast to the lifestyle of the believer. There will be no comparison. But it is not yet so. As the world has gotten worse, so have the standards of believers.

Purifying the Church

When I grew up, among fundamentalists there was a legalistic standard that said it was wrong to go to movies. In my teen years I would feel guilty if I went to a movie. Today we are asking ourselves if R-rated movies are acceptable. We have determined not to see X-rated films (newly dubbed NC-17), but R? Maybe. Yet today's movies are filled with sensuality! When we fill our minds with sensual images, we become corrupt. Our standards have gone down so that God must begin His judgment with the Church. If judgment must fall on the world, it must begin with the people of God. That is what we will see in the next few years, the purifying of the people of God. God is determined to draw the line between His Kingdom manifestation in the Body of believers and the kingdom of the god of this world, satan. This will be manifested in the unbelievers' lawlessness, in New Age foolishness, and in "anything goes" relativistic religion.

This is the principle of lawlessness. It is already in the world and it will come in fullness.

The Contrast Will Intensify

The picture of the Last Days in these Thessalonian chapters is not that the world is getting better because of our influence through the Gospel. It is a picture in which believers and the world become sharply separated, but in which unbelievers are such a mess that we can reap a great harvest among them! Many will recognize that they need the Gospel. Those who do not accept the Gospel will stay in delusion. Then there will be an incredible clash between good and evil. The battle will purify us and lead to the return of the Lord as well. That is the picture painted in Second Thessalonians 2.

Judgment Begins in the House of God

We would like to influence society for righteousness. But we must take care of our own house. Leaders in the Body of believers are living in secret adultery. Some leaders have divorced their wives and married others without biblical grounds. Yet they are still being received. They publicly preach on blood covenants! Judgment must begin with the people of God. Paul said that in the Last Days men *"shall be lovers of self, disobedient to parents, and lawless."* So it is.

The Resurrection and the Millennium

But [Messiah] *has indeed been raised from the dead, the firstfruits of those who have fallen asleep. For since death came through a man, the resurrection of the dead comes also through a man. For as in Adam all die, so in Christ all will be made alive. But each in his own turn:* [Messiah], *the firstfruits; then, when he comes, those who belong to him. Then the end will come, when he hands over the kingdom to God the Father after he has destroyed all dominion, authority and power.*

1 Corinthians 15:20-24

I think the implication here is that after the millennial age, Yeshua will deliver the Kingdom to God the Father. He puts an end to all other rule and authority and power.

*For he must reign until he has put all his enemies under
his feet.*   1 Corinthians 15:25

Postmillennialists say that He is reigning through the
Church, and we keep conquering until He puts all His enemies
under His feet. I see more of a cataclysmic end with His coming
to reign. The last enemy that will be destroyed is death. Death ends
for us when we receive our resurrection bodies, but death ultimately ends when the new heavens and the new earth come.

*I declare to you, brothers, that flesh and blood cannot
inherit the kingdom of God, nor does the perishable inherit the imperishable. Listen, I tell you a mystery. We
will not all sleep, but we will all be changed—in a flash,
in the twinkling of an eye, at the last trumpet. For the
trumpet will sound, the dead will be raised imperishable, and we will be changed. For the perishable must
clothe itself with the imperishable, and the mortal with
immortality. When the perishable has been clothed with
the imperishable, and the mortal with immortality, then
the saying that is written will come true: "Death has
been swallowed up in victory."*   1 Corinthians 15:50-54

Later we are given a motivation for knowing about the Last
Days:

*Therefore, my dear brothers, stand firm. Let nothing
move you. Always give yourselves fully to the work of
the Lord, because you know that your labor in the Lord
is not in vain.*   1 Corinthians 15:58

The Time Is Not Long to God

*I want you to recall the words spoken in the past by
the holy prophets and the command given by our Lord
and Savior through your apostles. First of all, you must*

understand that in the last days scoffers will come, scoffing and following their own evil desires. They will say, "Where is this 'coming' he promised? Ever since our fathers died, everything goes on as it has since the beginning of creation." But they deliberately forget that long ago by God's word the heavens existed and the earth was formed out of water and by water. By these waters also the world of that time was deluged and destroyed. By the same word the present heavens and earth are reserved for fire, being kept for the day of judgment and destruction of ungodly men.   2 Peter 3:2-7

You could look at the fire in different ways. I believe it is parallel to the fiery judgments of the Book of Revelation when the wrath of God is poured out.

But do not forget this one thing, dear friends. With the Lord a day is like a thousand years, and a thousand years are like a day.   2 Peter 3:8

Some have looked at history as a week of millennia. The first two thousand years from creation to Abraham, and the second from Abraham to Yeshua. The third two thousand years is from Yeshua until the Second Coming. That brings us to six thousand years, and the millennial age completes seven thousand. Does that help us to know the day when the Lord is coming? I don't think so. We have Usher's chronology. By his chronology we are nearing the year 6000. By Jewish chronology, only 5,749 years have gone by, so we have another 250 years to go. Although that is interesting, I don't think it is very helpful. We really cannot predict accurately.

God Is Patient With Humankind

The Lord is not slow in keeping his promise, as some understand slowness. He is patient with you, not

wanting anyone to perish, but everyone to come to
repentance.   2 Peter 3:9

The reason for the delay is so that all should come to repentance, so that the Body can have a time of restoration and an adequate witness to and calling of people from all nations. As we have
said, at the end the world comes to the knowledge of God. We want
to save as many as possible, for after the wrath of God has been
poured out, only a remnant will be left throughout the world. That
remnant will come to the knowledge of God and see the millennial promises. Millions will die in the fires of God's judgment. We
want to see people saved before that.

The Judgment Will Come

But the day of the Lord will come like a thief. The heav-
ens will disappear with a roar; the elements will be de-
stroyed by fire, and the earth and everything in it will be
laid bare.   2 Peter 3:10

This sounds a lot like Joel 2. Some people say that Peter is
talking about the end of this age, leading to the final new heavens
and the new earth. You can see how the amillennialist would say that
the end of this age is the end of the earth. Once again, you must understand that this passage speaks in what is known as the "apoca-
lyptic language," highly charged and symbolic. When Israel went
into exile, the prophets said that the stars fell from Heaven. This
could be the judgment before the Millennium as well. I think it is.
However, the language is very charged. The millennial age is a
new heaven and a new earth, but not in the final sense. It is described in Isaiah as an age of peace, prosperity, and longevity in
which people live an amazing number of years, but are still born,
marry, have children, and die.

*Since everything will be destroyed in this way, what
kind of people ought you to be? You ought to live holy
and godly lives as you look forward to the day of God
and speed its coming. That day will bring about the destruction of the heavens by fire, and the elements will
melt in the heat.*   2 Peter 3:11-12

In other words, our righteous lives hasten the coming of the
day of God.

*But in keeping with his promise we are looking forward to
a new heaven and a new earth, the home of righteousness.*
                                                          2 Peter 3:13

The New Heavens and New Earth

The Scriptures tell us there will be both new heavens and a
new earth. I believe, however, that the phrase "new heavens and
new earth" does not always speak about the ultimate new heavens
and new earth. In Isaiah 66 the language is not so precise and sci-
entific. I think Peter, in trying to deal with the issue of the Millennium, introduces it as a new heaven and a new earth. Maybe he
looks to the ultimate goal and leaves out the Millennium. Even if
you are an amillennialist, you can see Israel's salvation at the end
of this age leading immediately to the ultimate new heavens and
new earth. Living in godliness, fulfilling the John 17 prayer, and
realizing our destiny in God hastens the coming of the Day of the
Lord. The fulfillment of all our hopes is intertwined with our fulfilling the purposes of God. That is motivation indeed!

CHAPTER 4

THE SECOND COMING AND REVIVAL

by Keith Intrater

The Desire for Yeshua to Come Back

The desire of God's people to see Yeshua return to earth to rule and reign is a central theme of the Scriptures. Yeshua as the Messiah is portrayed as a Bridegroom, while we as His people are portrayed as a Bride. In the Spirit of God, there is a passionate desire on the part of both Yeshua and the Body of believers to come back together.

And the Spirit and the bride say, "Come!"

Revelation 22:17a

We are like a Bride who has been separated from her husband for many years and yearns to have him come back. Yeshua Himself likewise has a burning desire to come to us.

Revival and the Second Coming

There is a relationship between the occurrence of a mighty end-times revival and the coming of the Messiah. One affects the other. What we do on earth as believers affects the Second Coming. We have an involvement in the end-times events that culminate in Yeshua's return. Through faith and prayer and evangelism, we have a part to play. What we do, in a certain sense, hastens the day of His coming (2 Pet. 3:12).

A revival in the Last Days will set the stage and usher in the Messiah's return. In reverse, the awareness of Yeshua's imminent return and our meditating on the coming Day of the Lord causes us to be stirred up and motivated to the point where we are ready to receive that revival.

> *But know this, that if the master of the house had known what hour the thief would come, he would have watched and not allowed his house to be broken into. Therefore you also be ready, for the Son of Man is coming at an hour you do not expect.* Luke 12:39-40

> *I came to send fire on the earth, and how I wish it were already kindled!* Luke 12:49

Yeshua is desirous of coming back to us. He has fire with Him to kindle upon the earth. The more we are aware of that, the more we will be shaken out of our complacency. The more we focus our attention on His coming, the more we will stir ourselves to be alert, clean, and ready to receive. That readiness to receive opens the door for revival.

So the pattern is as follows: revelation of the Second Coming causes readiness to receive, which causes revival to break out, which ushers in the Second Coming.

Wake Up and Shake Up

The fact that Jesus is coming back soon and that the Day of the Lord is at hand is a terribly motivating factor. Take a moment to think how close Yeshua's return really is. That thought will stir you. What would you say, for example, if you knew that Yeshua would be coming back in exactly forty-eight hours? How would that affect you? It would certainly change your schedule. You would not likely go home and spend that forty-eight hours watching television.

If a certain man is employed at a job, the presence of the employer brings him into accountability. There is something about hearing the footsteps of the boss coming down the hallway. At the sound of those footsteps, the man is suddenly awake, sitting up straight, and busily engaged in the most serious matters.

It is like the housewife who rushes around the house to get everything in tip-top shape when she gets a sudden call that her mother-in-law is about to pay an unexpected visit.

Now these are carnal examples. Our level of motivation and integrity should be much higher than that. But the fact is that the imminent presence of the one who is your master tends to shake you out of complacency and instill in you a sense of urgency. So does the Lord's return energize our spiritual alertness and zeal.

The Baptism of Fire

He [Yeshua] *will baptize you with the Holy Spirit and fire.*   Matthew 3:11b

I believe this fire refers to a spiritual outpouring and revival that takes place right before the return of the Lord. The glory fire of God not only causes revival, but also purifies the people of God from sin and causes judgments to fall on the world systems. The coming of the Lord, the great and terrible Day of the Lord, is ushered in by fire. It is this baptism of fire that immediately precedes the second coming of Jesus.

We have a cooperative involvement in the coming of the Lord. As with almost all of God's works on earth, man has a part to play. To think it is all up to man is incorrect. That is a humanistic performance mentality. On the other hand, it is incorrect to assume God will merely intervene out of His independent omnipotence. That is religious passivity.

For we are God's fellow workers; you are God's field.
1 Corinthians 3:9

We then, as workers together with Him also plead with you not to receive the grace of God in vain.
2 Corinthians 6:1

So we have a cooperative relationship with God. We preach the gospel; He does the saving. We lay hands on the sick; He does the healing. We sow the seeds and water; He supplies the growth. So is the pattern in all God's operations. Therefore, God's people are involved in the events surrounding the Second Coming.

Surely the Lord GOD does nothing, unless He reveals His secret to His servants the prophets.   Amos 3:7

Can two walk together, unless they are agreed? Amos 3:3

When God is about to act and move upon the earth in judgment and deliverance, He generally moves first to reveal the plan to His people who are praying; then He seeks to bring them into cooperative faith agreement.

As God shared and discussed with Abraham His plans to visit Sodom and Gomorrah with judgment fire, so will He seek to share His plan with His children on earth concerning the baptism of fire during the endtimes. The closer we walk with God in obedient friendship and fellowship, the more we will be included in His counsel of operations.

The Last Word

The New Covenant Scriptures end with a statement by Yeshua and an affirmative response by John on behalf of God's people.

He who testifies to these things says, "Surely I am coming quickly." Amen. Even so, come, Lord Jesus!
Revelation 22:20

This is Yeshua's parting statement. It is His final declaration. It is a concise summary of His intention. John's brief prayer is the focal point of desire of the Church at large. It is a declaration of loyalty and faithfulness on the part of the Bride as she looks forward to the return of her husband. It is an acceptance of betrothal. Nothing else can come between us.

Yeshua's return and our fidelity to Him are a matter of oath-sworn covenant. It cannot be broken. From this parting comment we launched into the history of the New Covenant epoch.

Love as Strong as Death

We are praying for Him to return. He is desirous of returning. Our prayers and ministry endeavors are focused around this goal. The bonding between us and our Lord is like that of betrothed lovers.

I am my beloved's, and my beloved is mine.
Song of Solomon 6:3

I am my beloved's, and his desire is toward me.
Song of Solomon 7:10

The theme of the Song of Solomon is the desire of the betrothed lovers to be united with one another. It may be seen as an expression of the desire of the Church to see Yeshua return as her husband, and of His desire as well. This kind of loving passion is so strong that it will even defeat the last enemy, which is death (1 Corinthians 15:26). The love of the Messiah and His Bride is stronger than death itself. As our passion for Yeshua grows stronger and as the time of His return draws near, that lover's desire in Him and in us will release a fire on earth that will destroy every evil and conquer every stronghold.

For love is as strong as death, jealousy as cruel as the grave; its flames are flames of fire, a most vehement flame.
Song of Solomon 8:6

The baptism of fire is released out of our jealous love: ours for Yeshua, His for us. We will experience conquering authority over the forces of satan and death as our passion for Yeshua's return grows stronger.

Hastening the Day

God moves on the hearts of His people. They, in turn, begin to pray. That prayer changes and affects circumstances and events upon the earth. However, certain events are due to take place. They are pre-scheduled by prophetic Scriptures.

But these events do not take place in a vacuum. They happen as God moves upon the hearts of His prophetic people and those people begin to pour out intercessory prayer.

> *What manner of persons ought you to be in holy conduct and godliness, looking for and hastening the coming of the day of God, because of which the heavens will be dissolved, being on fire, and the elements will melt with fervent heat?* 2 Peter 3:11-12

How is it that we can hasten the coming of the Lord? What is it that we do to cause His return? How do we set in motion the chain of events that culminate in His coming? The events have already been prophesied to take place, but we put them in gear by our intercessory prayer and acts of obedience to the Lord.

Dynamics of Intercession

When ancient Israel was taken captive by the Babylonians, Jeremiah prophesied that they would return in seventy years (Jer. 25:11-12). Seventy years later, Daniel read the writings of Jeremiah that the time was at hand for the children of Israel to return (Dan. 9:2-3). But Daniel did not assume the events would take place automatically. He took the prophecy of Jeremiah as a direct mandate to get involved in the process by intercessory prayer.

Although Daniel saw that the prophetic timetable and sequence of events were already laid out, he did not take a fatalistic attitude toward it. Nor did he see himself as a curiosity seeker, watching with fascination as the events unfurled. His emphasis was not on sequence and schemes, even though he was quite aware that the timetables were there. Rather, his emphasis centered on generating a positive spiritual force through prayer that would help these prophecies be fulfilled.

So today our focus should not be on observing the times but rather, through discerning the times, on applying ourselves to appropriate intercession and involvement. We are not interested in end-times schemes of themselves, but only through them to be aware of the dynamics and strategies of the spiritual warfare in which we are engaged.

Baptism of Fire

The Bible indicates that the world is about to undergo a widespread baptism (immersion) in fire. This fire will engulf the world in the same manner that water engulfed the world in the time of Noah (2 Pet. 3:6-7). John the Baptist hinted at these two worldwide baptisms when he said that he would baptize in water first and then Yeshua would come to baptize in the Holy Spirit and in fire (Matt. 3:11).

Yeshua said He has great desire or zeal to see this fire come upon the earth. We want to enter into the same motivation that Yeshua has for this fire to come. First, we must understand why He desires this fire. This baptism of fire is related to His second coming.

John truly baptized with water, but you shall be baptized with the Holy Spirit not many days from now.

Acts 1:5

Symbolically, John's baptism with water may be seen as parallel to Noah's flood while Yeshua's baptism with the Spirit may be seen as parallel to the end-times immersion of fire. Yeshua's disciples saw the outpouring of God's Spirit connected with the time of establishing His Kingdom on earth (as well as intricately connected with the restoration of Israel as a sovereign nation).

Therefore...they asked Him, saying, "Lord, will You at this time restore the kingdom to Israel?" Acts 1:6

Yeshua is trying to talk to them about the outpouring of the Holy Spirit and how that outpouring will bring about His Kingdom. They want to talk about prophetic timetables and end-times schemes.

It is not for you to know times or seasons which the Father has put in His own authority. But you will receive power when the Holy Spirit has come upon you; and you shall be witnesses to Me in Jerusalem, and in all Judea and Samaria, and to the end of the earth.

Acts 1:7-8

Yeshua acknowledges that the Father has set specific times and seasons. But Yeshua directs His disciples to emphasize the Holy Spirit power rather than times. Yeshua accepts the premise that the establishment of the Kingdom involves the restoration of Israel, but again He directs their emphasis to being witnesses first in Israel and then around the world.

We should desire the coming of the Lord's Kingdom. That is the central thrust of the Lord's Prayer in Matthew 6: *"Your kingdom come."* Our priorities are: first, being filled with the power of the Holy Spirit; second, fostering revival in Jerusalem and Israel; and third, preaching the Gospel all over the world.

Peter said we could hasten the coming of Yeshua's kingdom (2 Pet. 3:12). As we dedicate ourselves to the power of the Holy Spirit, revival in Jerusalem, and evangelism around the world, we will be involved in our part of God's end-times plan.

In Like Manner

It was in the middle of this discussion that Yeshua was lifted up and taken to Heaven. An angel spoke to the astonished disciples and gave them a significant principle having to do with Yeshua's return.

This same Jesus, who was taken up from you into heaven, will so come in like manner as you saw Him go into heaven. Acts 1:11

Certainly Yeshua will come back down out of Heaven to the Mount of Olives. But there is more to it than that. For Yeshua to come back to that same place under similar historical circumstances, massive changes would have to take place in the demographic and political situation that has reigned over the Middle East during most of the past two thousand years. Amazingly enough, most of those changes have already taken place in our own times, creating a social and religious climate in many ways similar to that of the first century.

If Yeshua is to come back in like manner, like situations must occur. Truly, those situations are being restored before our very eyes. It is as if a giant motion picture of history is being rolled backwards to give us a situation of "like manner" for Yeshua to come back in.

The Jewish people are back in the land. There are secular Israelis like the fishermen and carpenters of Yeshua's day. There are orthodox Jews like the scribes and Pharisees. There are messianic Jews like the original believers in Yeshua. The world powers of Grecia, Magog, Babylon, and Persia are realigning themselves today. These are not exact duplicates, but they are similar enough to produce a spiritual equivalent.

The Book of Acts Reversed

I believe that "in like manner" can also refer to the general set of events in the Book of Acts and the sweep of religious history. The framework of the twentieth century is being rolled back in like manner to the first. The pattern of evangelism starting at Jerusalem and spreading to the ends of the earth is now being shifted from the ends of the earth back toward Israel and the Jewish people.

The major waves of events in the Book of Acts are rolling backwards like a countdown toward Acts 1. After Yeshua ascended to Heaven, a period of intercessory prayer culminated in the outpouring of the Spirit at Pentecost (*Shavuot*). This created a controversial revival in Jerusalem, accompanied by increasing persecution and tribulation. This led to the dispersing of the Jews out of the land of Israel, which, since the messianic Jews were among them, was accompanied by the spread of the gospel around the world. Empires rose and fell according to spiritual influences.

To put these in reverse order would give us a general pattern:

Stage E—Worldwide evangelism with realignment of international political powers.

Stage D—Regathering of the Jews, restoration of Israel, and a restoration movement in the Body of Christ.

Stage C—Intercession, persecution, tribulation, signs and wonders, revival refocusing toward Jerusalem.

Stage B—Fire of God falling, accompanied by glory and destruction.

Stage A—The return of the Messiah.

This is not a scheme of exact details but simply a pattern of spiritual causes and effects. As believers, we are to have a general awareness that where the carcass is the vultures will gather (Luke 17:37), that when the fig tree and other trees are ripe our redemption is near (Luke 21:30-31), and that Yeshua is returning "in like manner."

Parallel Restoration

It is also worth nothing that there is a parallel between the history of the nation of Israel and the life of Yeshua their Messiah. Yeshua and the life of Israel are connected. In the case when the anointed king David sinned, the whole nation suffered. When Jehoiachin was raised out of captivity, so the status of the nation of Israel was raised with him (2 Kings 25:27). So it is that the destiny of Israel is ultimately determined by the suffering and resurrection of her Messiah.

Yeshua's descent as a baby with Joseph and Miriam (Mary) into Egypt at the time of Herod was seen as a parallel to the events of Israel as a baby nation in the time of Moses (Matt. 2:15). When Yeshua was rejected, He knew that Israel would likewise be destroyed (Matt. 23:37-39). The death and torment of Yeshua is parallel to the two-thousand-year dispersion of the nation of Israel. The resurrection of Yeshua is modeled in the present-day restoration of the Jews to the land of Israel.

A parallel also exists between the history of Israel and the spiritual history of the Body of true believers in Yeshua. The dispersion of the Jews brought the spread of the gospel. Persecution of the Jews brought spiritual darkness to the Church. The restoration of the Hebrew language marked the restoration of speaking in tongues. The restoration of the nation of Israel is parallel to the various "restoration" movements in the Church today. Anti-Zionism and anti-Semitism are parallel to antichrist spirits.

A Second Pentecost

The great turning point of the Book of Acts is the outpouring of the glory of God upon the believers in Jerusalem in Acts 2.

I believe a similar outpouring of spiritual fire in Jerusalem and around the world will be the key turning point of the endtimes.

As we read Acts 2:1-5, notice the three elements that we refer to as the three primary foundations God is restoring to the Body of believers in these endtimes. They are: (1) integrity and covenant in relationships, (2) word of faith and Holy Spirit power, and (3) restoration of Israel and the Jewish roots of the faith. These three streams of revelation must be brought together as a strong threefold cord if God's will is to be accomplished among us.

> *When the Day of Pentecost had fully come, they were all with one accord in one place. And suddenly there came a sound from heaven, as of a rushing mighty wind, and it filled the whole house where they were sitting. Then there appeared to them divided tongues, as of fire, and one sat upon each of them. And they were all filled with the Holy Spirit and began to speak with other tongues, as the Spirit gave them utterance. And there were dwelling in Jerusalem Jews, devout men, from every nation under heaven.*   Acts 2:1-5

The Day of Pentecost is the ancient biblical Feast of Weeks, or *Shavuot*. It is not a coincidence that the outpouring of the Spirit took place on this day. God established the feasts as a pattern and format around which to release great movements of the Holy Spirit. The spring feasts were the pattern for God's plan of redemption in the first century. The autumn feasts are the pattern for God's plan of restoration in the last century.

If the Body of believers is to move with the flow of the Spirit in the endtimes, we must have an awareness of the role of the feasts of Israel and the foundations laid in the Law and the prophets.

The Jewish people being regrafted into the olive tree of faith (Rom. 11) is a central part of the restoration of the Body of believers in our time.

Covenant Relationships and Unity

Covenant relationships and integrity are demonstrated by the fact that the first-century believers were in one place (unity), in one accord (love), and that they were praying (holiness) under the direction of the apostles (congregational authority). Obviously, if we cannot act in unity, love, purity, and authority, we are not going to experience the glory of God.

The relationship between our unity and the glory of God has been pointed out by many in reference to John 17:22, where Yeshua prays that we might receive the same glory God gave to Him and that we would all be one.

The Dry Bones

The rushing sound of wind and fire is a sign of the outpouring of the Holy Spirit throughout the Scriptures. Of the many instances of God's glory and power moving like fire, wind, and storm, I think there is a particular parallel here to the "Dry Bones" prophecy of Ezekiel 37. The sound of wind in Acts 2 is like the sound of wind that brought the bones together and back to life as Ezekiel prophesied.

There again, the bones coming together stands for unity; the wind bringing them back to life is the power of the Holy Spirit; and the overall context is that of the restoration of the Jewish people. In a way, Acts 2 can be seen as an initial fulfillment of Ezekiel's vision.

The Two Sticks

It is also no coincidence that the dry bones prophecy of Ezekiel 37 leads to another prophecy of the two sticks of Israel and Judah being joined together (Ezek. 37:16 ff.). This symbolic prophecy can be applied on several different levels, but they are all to be seen as a result and integral part of the great outpouring of the Holy Spirit in the endtimes.

In context, the two sticks represent a healing of the division between the northern and southern kingdoms at the time of Solomon's son Rehoboam in 931 B.C. (2 Kings 12). So the two sticks coming together represent the preservation and integrity of the Jewish nation as a whole.

The two sticks may also be seen as a healing and unity movement within the Body of believers. (Obviously we are speaking of a supernatural spiritual unity of the Holy Spirit and not in any way of a manmade ecumenicism.)

Thirdly, the two sticks may be seen as a healing of the divisive history between the Church and the Jews. It may be seen in the unity of Jewish believers and Gentile believers within the Body of Christ (Eph. 2:14-15). It may even be seen as the hope for a more unified government among the political parties in Israel today.

Finally, the two sticks may be seen as God's desire to heal any division among the messianic Jewish believers themselves. Let us pray for the outpouring of God's Spirit as shown in Ezekiel 37 and Acts 2, and that the outpouring will result in healing and restoration of God's people in all walks of life.

Infilling of the Spirit and Prophecy

Returning to Acts 2, we note, of course, that the most important part of the passage is that the believers are filled with the Holy Spirit (v. 4). As they are, they begin to speak out in tongues and prophetic utterances. Whenever someone is filled with the Holy Spirit, he will break forth in utterances of praise and prophecy, because out of the abundance of the heart the mouth speaks (Matt. 12:34).

The release of prophetic utterances and the gifts of the Holy Spirit led to revival in the streets of Jerusalem. So it was in the case of Ezekiel; as he prophesied and *because* he prophesied, the dry bones came alive and came together. It is the move of the Spirit of God and the prophetic cooperation of God's people that give birth to the Kingdom of God upon this earth. It is crucial for the Body of believers to understand this powerful dynamic.

The Holy Spirit works with us in each stage as we move from repentance to revival to restoration. As we are filled with God's Spirit and speak out prophetically in faith, the Holy Spirit moves on the earth to create the events that gave birth to the Kingdom of God. Our prayer, our relationships with one another, the infilling of the Holy Spirit, the gifts of the Spirit, the restoration of Israel and the Jewish roots of Christianity, revival, evangelism, and the restoration of the Church all have to do with bringing about Yeshua's return and the Kingdom of God on earth. These elements are like pieces of a jigsaw puzzle that God is putting together, bringing everything back under His will at the fullness of time (Eph. 1:10).

Showdown in Jerusalem

In Acts 2:5-41 we see that there are devout Jews in Jerusalem from every nation. The three thousand people who were saved on Pentecost morning were orthodox Jews who had come up to Jerusalem to celebrate the biblical feast of *Shavuot*. Three thousand orthodox Jews in Jerusalem getting saved in one morning is hard for us to fathom. Today, as back then, Jews lived in every nation and would come from afar to Jerusalem for special worship occasions.

The outpouring of the Holy Spirit resulted in confrontation between the Jewish believers in Yeshua and the orthodox Jews. In a certain sense, revival always brings confrontation between the new fanatics and the established religious organizations. Whoever wants to walk in the power of the Holy Spirit must be ready to handle that conflict.

Although the outpouring of the Spirit produces this challenge between revival and religious authorities in any location, there is a significant meaning to this happening in Jerusalem between the Jewish believers and the orthodox religious establishment. That same conflict caused Yeshua to be crucified and also surrounded the birth of the Kingdom of God in the first century. I believe the outpouring of the Holy Spirit on Jewish believers in the face of the Jewish community in Jerusalem is a central event that will help usher in the second coming of Yeshua.

The spiritual battle over the souls of Jerusalem is the last great showdown between the forces of good and evil. Here signs and wonders and pillars of smoke will take place immediately before the great and awesome Day of the Lord (Acts 2:19-20). The forces of satan will be faced and defeated. Yeshua will intervene to establish His reign. Souls will be saved. Victory in this conflict will require the avid intercession of almost every Spirit-filled believer on the face of the earth. It will be like a great birth pang before the delivery. Can you hear that in your heart?

A Restored Church

Although the world system around us will grow more evil in the endtimes, we as the people of God will be growing more pure and bright. As society and culture around us turn against God, they will begin to persecute the true believers even more viciously. But in the midst of that attack, we will grow stronger spiritually. The Church, or Bride, that Yeshua is coming back for is described as glorious and without any spot or blemish (Eph. 5:27).

While the pagan nations of the world may turn against Israel (Zech. 14:2), a greater unity and mutual understanding will develop between Jew and Gentile within the Body of Christ (Eph. 2:14). False Christianity will fall prey to spirits of anti-Semitism and anti-Zionism, but the believers will develop a greater awareness of the Jewish roots of the faith (Rom. 11).

Power is released in the Body of believers when we enter into cooperation between Jew and Gentile. As the correct interaction between male and female provides zest and romance within a marriage, so does the distinctive relationship between Jew and Gentile provide spiritual dynamism within a New Covenant congregation. Wisdom and revelation will flow as we bring out of our treasure and heritage things new and old (Matt. 13:52).

The Two Prerequisites

We have the twofold commission to see evangelism spread to all the people in the world who do not know the Lord, and to see restoration and fullness among those who do know the Lord. This dual commission is a prerequisite for the return of Yeshua.

> *And this gospel of the kingdom will be preached in all the world as a witness to all the nations, and then the end will come.* Matthew 24:14

Worldwide evangelism comes before Yeshua comes back. That is our part in the Second Coming. One of the reasons for witnessing is to promote Yeshua's return.

> *O Jerusalem, Jerusalem, the one who kills the prophets and stones those who are sent to her! How often I wanted to gather your children together, as a hen gathers her chicks under her wings, but you were not willing. See! Your house is left to you desolate; for I say to you, you shall see Me no more till you say, "Blessed is He who comes in the name of the Lord!"* Matthew 23:37-39

Yeshua said He would not return to Jerusalem until she welcomed Him back with a blessing. In other words, Yeshua is not returning to the earth until Jerusalem's heart has turned to accept

Him. Or, to put it in a positive light, as soon as the people in Jerusalem receive Yeshua as their Lord, He will return.

Zion in Your Heart

That is why there is such an intense spiritual battle connected with Jewish evangelism. Satan knows that this is his last stand. Yeshua has always wanted to gather the Jews of Jerusalem under His wing, and He still does. The spiritual battle over this group of people has always caused God's messengers to be attacked. Let us pray for those who are particularly sent to bring this message to Jerusalem, and let us pray that she would be "willing" this time.

A messianic revival in Jerusalem is the final prerequisite for the Second Coming. As you are reading these words, you now have a part in it through faith agreement and intercession.

A word of caution: Many misguided attempts on behalf of Christians to "convert" Jews have at times made matters worse instead of better. In this important spiritual arena, all involvement should be done with a great deal of prayer, love, discernment, and specific direction from God.

Note: When Yeshua says "Jerusalem," He is referring not only to the population in the street but particularly to the government and religious authorities. Remember that the multitudes of Jewish people were attracted to Yeshua. It was the leaders who turned against Him out of jealousy. It is the equivalent of that group of priests and politicians whose hearts must be turned. Yeshua refers to Jerusalem the way we refer to Washington, meaning the authority that capital city stands for. In the case of Jerusalem, Yeshua is addressing both.

Our Involvement Counts

The prophecies of Scripture set forth God's absolute plan for the endtimes, which cannot be changed. However, within that overall structure are many variables that *can* be affected by our involvement in prayer and witnessing. Our involvement can have a positive effect, while our lack of involvement will have an adverse one.

For example, it is clear that God is going to bring the Jewish people out of Russia. Our prayer can cause them to come out voluntarily and with the cooperation of the government. Without prayer, many more of them will suffer great hardship, violence, and persecution.

Another example is the assurance that God will turn Israel's heart to Himself. With prayer, this can be accomplished with a greater degree of peace, love and health. Without prayer, it will be accomplished in the midst of more distress, pain and war.

God's plan will be accomplished, but the more people who cooperate with Him, the easier it will go for the inhabitants of earth. That is why God directed Paul to minister in areas where more people's hearts were receptive. (*"No one will attack you to hurt you; for I have many people in this city"*—Acts 18:10.) God's plan will go forward, but the degree to which the human race experiences grace or hardship depends on us.

The Acts 2 Model

The outpouring of God's Spirit on the believers in Acts 2 was a fulfillment of prophecies from the Book of Joel, but it was not the final fulfillment of those prophecies. The Book of Joel is referring to cataclysmic events that take place immediately before *"the great and terrible day of the Lord."* As the Acts 2 Pentecostal experience was the primary breakthrough of the Spirit at the birth of the Church, it stands today as our model and archetype for the great revival of the endtimes, both in Jerusalem and around the world.

This is what was spoken by the prophet Joel: "And it shall come to pass in the last days, says God, that I will pour out of My Spirit on all flesh."   Acts 2:16-17

Peter and those early messianic believers experienced a mighty blast of what Joel was speaking of. But the full cataclysm of God's power is yet impending and about to be released on this generation. We might say that the best (and worst) is yet to come. The Acts 2 experience is our standard for what "will come to pass in the last days."

I will show wonders in heaven above and signs in the earth beneath: blood and fire and vapor of smoke. The sun shall be turned into darkness, and the moon into blood, before the coming of the great and awesome day of the LORD.   Acts 2:19-20

What happened in Acts 2 will happen again in our day but in an even greater dimension. All the signs of blood and fire and glory were not completed in the first century. They have been continuing on to a certain degree in revivals throughout the centuries, but they are about to culminate in a way that will shake the world with the power of God.

The Theme of Joel

When Peter preached on that Pentecost (*Shavuot*) morning, he quoted from the Book of Joel. He saw them doing what Joel had prophesied. Joel speaks of extended periods of intercession, which is exactly what the believers were doing before the fire fell. It seems consistent with the Spirit of God that during the believers' prayer times, the Holy Spirit directed them to meditate on Joel's prophecies. Their hearts were so full of the revelations therein that they identified themselves with what Joel prophesied.

They were, in a certain sense, motivated by the force of the content of that book. And what is that content? The earth-shaking events that take place immediately before the coming of the Lord. The revelation of the coming of the Lord spurred them on to intensive intercession. That intercession led to a miraculous revival that shook the world.

In our time, the same pattern will reoccur, but on such a wide scale that it will actually prompt in the coming of the Lord. The Book of Joel is significant because it relates the Acts 2 experience with the second coming of Yeshua. It ties together the three elements in a chain reaction: (1) intensive intercession, (2) an earth-shaking revival in the midst of disastrous world events, and (3) the return of Yeshua.

It seems likely that since Yeshua gave the disciples detailed instructions prior to their prayer and revival, He must have been the one to direct them toward this passage in Joel. I believe that today as well He is directing us to the same spiritual dynamics to foster a revival that will result in His return.

How Will This Happen?

How will we see the second coming of Yeshua? By participating in a world-scale revival. How will we see revival? By participating in intensive intercession. How will we be motivated for intercession? By meditating on the second coming of Yeshua and desiring it. As we get zealous for revival and the Kingdom of God, it hastens the day of His coming (2 Pet 3:12).

Of course the world system will not let this happen without a fight. The forces of evil despise the light. The more we go forward with God's plan, the more nasty and vicious will be the persecution directed at us. Satan knows his time is short, so he is spitting and scratching like a cornered cat. Let us not be dismayed. The same glory cloud that brought deliverance and light to the Israelites brought darkness and destruction to the Egyptians (Ex. 14:20).

The Church and Israel

As the Church is restored in these endtimes, one key element that is being restored is her Jewish roots and the Jewish wing of the Body of believers. An important part of God's overall restoration is the return of the Jewish people to Israel and Israel's place among the nations.

God is restoring and bringing into position both the Church and Israel. They are supposed to work together as a team. In fact they will ultimately be grafted into one another. They will overlap one another. One place where they do overlap today is in the movement of Jewish believers in Yeshua, sometimes referred to as messianic Judaism. Jewish believers form the crucial link between the Church and Israel. How God longs for these two to cooperate and come together!

If restoration and revival in the Church is to be met with opposition from the world system of evil, it is equally true that the restoration of the nation of Israel will be met with opposition and attack from the community of nations. Is that not happening before our eyes? It is important that the Church recognize that international opposition to Israel comes from the same satanic source as the persecution of true believers. The Church, and particularly her prayer warriors, must not abandon her sister Israel as the times of distress mount in the coming years.

The same covenant of God with Abraham that promised a Savior to the world through his seed also promised the territory of Israel to Abraham's physical descendants. The attack against Israel's right to that property is ultimately an attack on the validity of the same covenant that brought us Yeshua as the Messiah. The

spirits of anti-Semitism and anti-Zionism are closely akin therefore to the spirits of antichrist.

An attack upon the Church, which is the Body of Christ, is
actually an attack upon Yeshua, who is the head of that body (Acts
9:4). Likewise, an attack upon Israel is actually an attack on
Yeshua, who is the King of Israel (John 19:19).

In Summary

God's plan is for a mighty revival to precede the second coming of Yeshua. That revival will take place in the midst of persecution and opposition from the world system. God's plan for
restoration includes the restoration of Israel, which will also be
met by persecution and attack but must not be abandoned by the
Church.

The element that ties all these factors together is a miraculous revival in Jerusalem among Jewish believers in Yeshua. This
revival will be patterned after the Acts 2 Pentecostal experience
but with even greater ramifications. This revival will also be accomplished in the midst of enormous tribulation.

This perspective should help us to understand more clearly
the events described in the Book of Revelation that highlight terrible tribulation, miraculous outpourings of God's Spirit, and a
central focus on the role of a Jewish remnant of believers in
Yeshua.

A Note of Irony

Just as revival in the Church is met with opposition from the
world systems, and just as the restoration of Israel is met with opposition from the community of nations, so is a revival movement
among Jewish believers in Yeshua also met with opposition from
the Jewish community and even at times from the Church. If the

restoration of Israel as a nation faces attack from the devil, how much more so will a revival of Jewish believers in Israel.

It is ironic that the very Jewish community which has been persecuted by the nations in turn persecutes the Jewish believers in her midst. The nation of Israel is beloved by God because of her forefathers and her gifts and callings, but she is often the enemy of the gospel (Rom. 11:28-29). The same God-hating spirit that makes the nations attack the Jews also makes the Jews attack the Jewish believers in Yeshua. The Romans oppressed the Jews while the Jews oppressed the Jewish believers.

True Christians must be aware of this spiritual dynamic. While they must support Israel in the face of the nations, how much more must they support Jewish believers in the face of Israel as a nation. If God desires restoration of Israel as a whole, how much more does He desire revival within that nation. Jesus is still the King of the Jews no matter who does not like the fact or who rejects it. Whether the nations reject Israel, whether the Jews reject Jesus, whether the world system persecutes the Church, whether the Church misunderstands the messianic Jews, whether Israel persecutes the messianic Jews, or whether the Church abandons Israel, He is still Lord. He is both King of kings and the King of the Jews.

The Terrible Day of the Lord

Let us examine a little more closely the prophecies of Joel, as they lay a foundation for end-times revival and the return of Yeshua. The Book of Joel conveys a yearning, much like the Book of Revelation, for Yeshua to come back; it also issues a warning about the difficulties that day entails.

Alas for the day! For the day of the LORD is at hand; it shall come as destruction from the Almighty. Joel 1:15

Blow the trumpet in Zion, and sound an alarm in My holy mountain! Let all the inhabitants of the land tremble; for the day of the LORD is coming, for it is at hand.

Joel 2:1

The day of the LORD is great and very terrible.

Joel 2:11

The sun shall be turned into darkness, and the moon into blood, before the coming of the great and awesome day of the LORD.   Joel 2:31

The final consummation of the war between good and evil on earth is the theme of Joel just as it is of John's revelation. On the one hand we are to desire it because it will bring the return of our beloved Messiah and the outward rule of God on the earth, but on the other hand we see it as a fearful time of judgment and tribulation.

A worldwide baptism of fire will take place in the endtimes. This fire will be an immersion in miraculous power and glory for the people of God. It will also mean worldwide disaster and destruction. This dual fire of judgment and glory is part of God's plan. Yeshua desires for it to take place. God wants His controversy with man and the devil brought to an end.

Dual Intercession

As the spiritual currents of the Book of Joel led to the outpouring at Pentecost (*Shavuot*), so will they in a parallel fashion lead to the worldwide baptism of fire in the Second Pentecost. The first element is that of intercession.

"Turn to Me with all your heart, with fasting, with weeping, and with mourning." So rend your heart, and not your garments. Blow the trumpet in Zion, consecrate a fast, call a sacred assembly.   Joel 2:12-13,15

This period of intercession may be taken on two levels. First, it is a picture of the Church turning to God in prayer, purifying her heart, identifying with the lost, and consecrating herself to God's will.

Secondly, it may be seen as the nation of Israel turning to God for mercy and military protection in the face of an onslaught by enemy nations. Again, much soul searching will take place as the people realize that without the intervention of God, they are in a hopeless situation. Mere human ability is failing.

One of the primary areas of intercession for the Church should be in praying for Israel's peace, both spiritually and physically (Ps. 122:6). The Jewish believers in Yeshua will find themselves involved in both Israel's struggle and that of the Church.

A trumpet is blowing in the spiritual realm to arouse our conscience and stir us to this prayer and consecration.

Focus on His Land

As God directs His attention to reestablishing the nation of Israel, the hearts of believers will pick up on His desire.

The LORD will be zealous for His land, and [have compassion on] *His people.*   Joel 2:18

The supernatural resurrection of the state of Israel has caused Christians all over the world to deal with the many prophecies concerning God's will for Israel. Israel's miraculous victories in war against overwhelming odds have also caused believers everywhere to discern the hand of God's protection through angelic armies. God is on the move and zealous; we need to be on the move and zealous with Him.

I will no longer make you a reproach among the nations.
                    Joel 2:19

When the Jewish people were scattered throughout the Gentile nations without a homeland of their own, they were despised.

As a nation, their condition was a reproach compared to other nations.

Today Israel is still considered a reproach in the international community due to communist, Islamic, and terrorist propaganda. The Body of believers has also suffered great reproach at the hands of a humanistic and anti-Christian media. God will not allow that much longer. While judgment begins with the house of God, it does go on and pass over the ungodly eventually.

The Northern Army

Because Israel is situated with a desert to the east and a sea to the west, whenever an army would attack they would always descend from the north. So armies as diverse as the Greeks to the Persians could be referred to as the "northern army." But in endtimes prophecy, the northern army is particularly referred to as Gog and Magog (Ezek. 38–39) and seems to indicate Russia and the nations directly to the north of Israel.

But I will remove far from you the northern army, and will drive him away into a barren and desolate land...because he has done monstrous things. Joel 2:20

So at a point which seems to be in the rather near future, God intervenes to turn back a military assault from the army of the north. In the 1984 war in Lebanon, Israel uncovered enough armaments to equip a major invasion. The arms were made, of course, in Russia.

It is important to note that this invasion and the defeat of the northern army is not part of the larger battle usually referred to as Armageddon (Joel 3, Zech. 14, and Rev. 19). This defeat of the northern army comes first, then there is a period of miraculous revival and tribulation, after which comes the larger battle.

In this first encounter, the devastation is not as great and the number of people involved is not as large. The first defeat will serve as a pretext and motivating factor for the northern armies' involvement in the second onslaught.

In the first invasion of the northern armies, the armies are defeated on the mountains of Israel (Ezek. 39:4). In the second invasion half the city of Jerusalem is destroyed (Zech. 14:2). It is in the second war that Jesus intervenes forcibly from Heaven (Zech. 14:3-4, Rev. 19:14).

The General Sequence

If we follow the sweep of Joel 2 and 3, a pattern emerges:

1. A movement of intercession and repentance (2:12-15)
2. A focus of attention on Israel's territorial claims (2:18)
3. A dealing with public reproach on the Church and Israel (2:19)
4. The initial defeat of the northern army (2:20)
5. A time of restoration for Israel (and figuratively, the Church) (2:21-26)
6. Miraculous revival and intense persecution (2:28-32)
7. The gathering of an international military assault on Israel (3:1-14)
8. The sudden gathering in of a divine army out of the sky (3:11)
9. An explosive and abrupt intervention by God at Jerusalem (3:16)
10. The establishment of a new paradise-style of life out of Israel (3:18)

This sequence of events fits well with our overall understanding of spiritual law and the battle between good and evil. It also fits well with the end-times descriptions found in Zechariah 12–14, Ezekiel 36–40, Revelation 6–20, and Jesus' end-times explanations in the gospels.

The Vine and the Fig Tree

After the northern army has been removed (v. 20), there follows a beautiful time of renewal and restoration (v. 21-27).

Fear not, O land; be glad and rejoice...Do not be afraid,
you beasts of the field... Joel 2:21-22

There is a particular emphasis on the land itself and the natural reserves. Israel will experience a time of economic and agricultural blessing.

The tree bears its fruit; the fig tree and the vine yield
their strength. Joel 2:22

Literally, this verse is speaking of agricultural prosperity within Israel. But it has a symbolic meaning as well. In the Gospels, the Body of believers is referred to as a vine (John 15) and Israel is referred to as a fig tree (Luke 21). They are pictured here as bearing fruit together.

This mutual fruit-bearing indicates a parallel restoration within the Church and Israel. A spiritual kinship exists between the two. God's will is for their cooperation and mutual support. They were designed to help one another prosper.

Note: It is interesting that Yeshua cursed a fig tree (Mark 11) when it was not the time for it to bear fruit. Now is the time for the fig tree to bear fruit, and God's blessing is upon it.

Material and Spiritual Blessings

Be glad then, you children of Zion, and rejoice in the
LORD your God; for He has given you the former rain
faithfully, and He will cause the rain to come down for
you—the former rain, and the latter rain in the first
month. Joel 2:23

Physically, rainfall in the Middle East is the source of agricultural growth and therefore economic prosperity. Spiritually,

133

rainfall represents the outpouring of God's Spirit in revival. Combining the former rain and the latter rain indicates a revival of such proportions that it will be a consummation of all the revivals that have gone before.

In the Bible, spiritual and material things are linked together. Forgiveness and healing are linked together, as well as revival and prosperity. Again we note that the destinies of the Church and Israel are married, as it were, to one another.

> *The threshing floors shall be full of wheat, and the vats shall overflow with new wine and oil.* Joel 2:24

Wheat, wine, and oil are all part of material prosperity in an agricultural society. Symbolically, wheat or bread stands for the teaching of the true Word of God, and new wine and oil stands for the joy and anointing power of the Holy Spirit.

> *I will restore to you the years that the swarming locust has eaten...* Joel 2:25

Once again we find a prophecy indicating God's plan for restoration, a restoration in the Church and a restoration in Israel, right in the midst of the end-times events.

Some say these prophecies refer only to restoration in the Church; others say they refer only to restoration in Israel. We see both the Church and Israel as manifestations of the same spirit of restoration that God is working upon the earth. God is, in fact, moving to restore all things (Acts 3:21) and bring all things under the leadership of the Messiah Himself (Eph. 1:10).

What Causes Tribulation?

The restoration of the Church and Israel takes place in the midst of the persecution and tribulation of the endtimes. This is not a coincidence. As God moves among His people, spiritual forces are stirred up. The world system of evil reacts and fights back. If God's people are not going forward in God's will, satan has little need for open attack.

For example, there was not much international outrage over Zionism when no Zionist movement existed. The positive and righteous actions of God's people provoke a negative and satanic reaction from the ungodly.

If the Church is lukewarm and Israel is not obeying God, the world will slip half asleep into death and perdition. To a certain degree, it is the manifest glory of God in the Church and Israel that causes the tribulations and persecutions of the endtimes. It is almost as if the Tribulation cannot occur unless the Church and Israel are in their respective positions in God's plan.

Why Revival Tarries

Joel's prophecy now moves onto a new stage. (Notice the word *afterward*.)

> *And it shall come to pass afterward that I will pour out*
> *My Spirit on all flesh; your sons and your daughters*
> *shall prophesy.*   Joel 2:28a

An outpouring of God's Spirit will take place after the events just described. This outpouring was what Peter said was happening in that first-century Pentecost and will happen again in our times on a wider scale. The outpouring will not take place until the other events occur beforehand.

What immediately precedes the spiritual outpouring is the mutual restoration of the Church and Israel just described. Again, this is no coincidence. God will not pour forth His Spirit until the Church and Israel are restored enough to receive it and bear testimony to the world.

Our love, unity, repentance, and intercession result in the removal of the northern army and the restoration of ministry in the Church, of the nation of Israel, and of the Body of Jewish believers in Yeshua. When that happens, and not until then, God's power and judgment and glory will be released.

We are seeing the beginning of these things take place right now. Ultimately, the same falling of the fire of God that took place in the Book of Acts will occur again, but this time it will happen not only to a group of Jewish believers in Jerusalem, but to a prepared Body of people all over the world.

Right now the foundations of prayer, prophetic ministry, and covenant integrity are being strengthened among believers around the world to give God legal grounds, as it were, to release His power. The Bride is being cleaned up. The foundations are being rebuilt so that righteousness can move into action.

On All Flesh

Yet God's Spirit is to be poured out not only on His children but on all flesh.

I will pour out My Spirit on all flesh; your sons and your daughters shall prophesy. Joel 2:28

Figuratively, it may be said that "all flesh" refers to everyone in the world, and "your sons and your daughters" refers to the believers and their families within the covenant community of faith. The Spirit will hit everybody but presumably with different results on different people.

As we believers dedicate ourselves to intercession, evangelism, and the supernatural operations of the Holy Spirit, the Spirit of God will pour out on us in glory. But the Spirit of God will also pour out through us in signs and wonders toward the unbelievers. We are spiritual people, and the Holy Spirit can move through our reborn spirits. As that happens, we minister the power of the Spirit in miracles and evangelism upon the lost. This gives them the opportunity to repent and receive, or to resist and rebel.

As the glory of God moves through us, the miraculous manifestations are signs of prophecy whereby we can minister in the supernatural. As the glory of God touches an unbeliever who is open to repent and receive salvation, the miraculous manifestations are signs for evangelism to them. As the glory of God touches someone who is hardened and unrepentant, the power of God will destroy them, and the miraculous manifestations will be signs of judgment.

It is the same glorious power of the Holy Spirit, but it has different effects depending on the heart condition of the person it touches.

Glory Versus Judgment

So the signs and wonders of the Last Days will in some ways be gloriously positive but in other ways horribly negative.

> *I will show wonders in the heavens and in the earth: blood and fire and pillars of smoke. The sun shall be turned into darkness, and the moon into blood, before the coming of the great and awesome day of the LORD.*
>
> Joel 2:30-31

These signs and wonders are described in detail in the Book of Revelation. Joel gives a brief prophetic summary here. Judgment on the world results in deliverance for the covenant people.

Just as it was in the time of the Exodus, the glory of God fell as horrible judgment on the pagan world system. The plagues of Exodus are parallel to the plagues of Revelation. The signs and wonders destroy the demonic principalities of the time. Those who worship pagan gods are destroyed with those gods. The covenant people are present during the time to bear witness of the truth. They are supernaturally protected and even prosper in the midst of judgment. Remember, while there was darkness in Egypt there was light in Goshen.

CHAPTER 5

LAST DAYS TRIBULATION

by Keith Intrater

Escalating Conflict

Miracles of deliverance must, of necessity, be matched by signs of judgment on the world. It has to be that way because the forces of evil have entrenched themselves in opposition to God's love.

> *When you hear of wars and rumors of wars, do not be troubled; for such things must happen, but the end is not yet.* Mark 13:7

There is a necessary series of cause and effect. As the people of God act, the world system reacts. Any manifestation of the Kingdom of God on earth is attacked and persecuted by evil. The confrontation between good and evil is unavoidable. The conflict escalates at each stage.

This pattern of escalating conflict is described in Yeshua's prophecy in Mark 13 as it is in Joel.

First the spiritual conflict is engaged with wars, political turnovers, earthquakes, famines, and troubles (v. 8). This is the beginning stage.

> *These are the beginnings of sorrows.* Mark 13:8

These natural disasters and social upheavals are accompanied by increasing evangelism on every continent, extending even to synagogues and political leaders (v. 9).

The gospel must first be preached to all the nations.

Mark 13:10

Again, it must happen this way. This increase of evangelism provokes a reaction of increased persecution and betrayal, even involving family members (vv. 11-12). The beginning of sorrows has escalated to greater tribulation.

You will be hated by all for My name's sake. But he who endures to the end shall be saved. Mark 13:13

Despite such opposition, God's people will be strengthened to endure and maintain their stand of faith all the way through this period to the end.

This period of trouble increases until it becomes the worst possible time in the history of man.

In those days there will be tribulation, such as has not been since the beginning of [time]. Mark 13:19

What limits and restrains the outpouring of God's wrath is the ability of the saints to maintain their faith. While God's will is to protect and prosper His people in the midst of these tribulations, it will be extremely difficult for them to endure.

The End of Tribulation

Traditional or lukewarm Christianity will collapse during this time. Everyone will be forced to be hot or cold: either ardently faithful or stubbornly resistant to God's voice of conscience. Many mainline denominations will take a stance of morality and theology that is completely opposed to God and His Word.

This fierce pressure will take place because God endeavors to save every single person possible and to destroy every demonic stronghold that has held the human race captive. Every form of sin and satanic activity will be rooted out so that no vestige whatsoever will remain in the new creation age.

*Unless the Lord had cut short those days, no flesh
would survive; but for the sake of God's elect people
whom He has chosen, He cut short those days.*

Mark 13:20 (my paraphrase)

God's people are here during this time as workers in the
greatest harvest of souls ever. But ultimately the time of tribulation is halted because the people of God have reached their absolute limit to endure.

Simply put, the Tribulation is a period of warfare between the
forces of good and evil. The wrath of God is a military action on
the part of the armies of heaven to rescue God's people on earth.
The saints of God must be there to participate in the battle and the
harvest. It is for the sake of God's people that He moves in judgment and power to deliver them. Finally, it is for their sake as well
that the time of wrath is cut short.

The Second Coming

This period of intense spiritual warfare and tribulation culminates in the last great outpouring (vv. 24-25), the coming of
Yeshua in power (v. 26), and the sweeping up of the saints into the
air by angels (v. 27).

*In those days, after that tribulation, the sun will be
darkened, and the moon will not give its light; the stars
of heaven will fall, and the powers in the heavens will
be shaken. Then they will see the Son of Man coming in
the clouds with great power and glory. And then He will
send His angels, and gather together His elect from the
four winds, from the farthest part of earth to the farthest
part of heaven.* Mark 13:24-27

When Yeshua speaks of the stars and powers of heaven being
shaken, He is referring to the same final outpouring of power that

we have been calling the Second Pentecost (described in Joel 2, Acts 2, and the Book of Revelation). Notice that it is *"in those days after that tribulation."* In other words, it comes at the end of the Tribulation period but is part of the same series of events. The powers of heaven being shaken denotes battle among the armies of angels and demons in the spiritual realm around us.

The Time Clock

While we are not overly concerned with time sequence, notice at least the following phrases:

Verse 24: After the Tribulation (comes the heaven shaking).

Verse 26: The the Son of Man returns.

Verse 27: His angels gather the elect in the air.

So the overall pattern in Mark 13 might be boiled down to the following:

1. Tribulation
2. Evangelism
3. More tribulation
4. Final outpouring
5. Yeshua coming
6. Saints gathered by angels

Once again, my point is not to show a specific scheme but to demonstrate the mutual cause-and-effect relationships between the events in Israel, the involvement of the Church, the persecution from the world system, the glory power on the Church, the judgment upon the world system, and the coming of Jesus.

> *Now learn this parable from the fig tree: When its branch has already become tender, and puts forth leaves, you know that summer is near. So you also, when you see these things happening, know that it is near—at the doors!*   Mark 13:28-29

Israel, or the fig tree, has been referred to as the time clock of the endtimes. Yeshua calls the events happening with the fig tree a parable, or what we might call a symbolic example. So Yeshua is saying that as events take place in the spiritual realm, believers are to discern the progress of these events by looking at certain indicators—prophetic events in the world at large and specifically those occurring in Israel.

What We Are to Know

Notice as well that Yeshua has commanded us to be aware of the progress of these events:

Verse 28: Know that summer is near.

Verse 29: Know that it is near.

Verse 33: Take heed and watch.

Verse 35: Watch therefore.

Verse 37: I say to all "Watch!"

The reason Yeshua describes the spiritual events of the endtimes, tells us to watch Israel as a timepiece, gives us spiritual principles to discern the times, and commands us to be alert is that He does not want us to be caught unaware at His coming. He does not want us to miss the role we are to play in the final harvest.

Lest, coming suddenly, he find you sleeping. Mark 13:36

Yeshua is commanding us to receive revelation concerning the endtimes, so that we can do our part and not be hurt ourselves. These prophecies are strategic instructions and battlefront information for His end-times army of saints.

What We Are Not to Know

While we are supposed to know the general sweep of events and the pattern of spiritual warfare, we are not to focus our attention on exact time schedules. There is a balance here.

Some people get so caught up with the minute details of end-times prophecy that they miss the mandate to intercede and evangelize. Others dismiss end-times prophecy as impossible to understand and are in the dark as to how they should direct their prayers and involvement.

Of that day and hour no one knows, not even the angels in heaven, nor the Son, but only the Father. Mark 13:32

Watch therefore, for you do not know when the master of the house is coming—in the evening, at midnight, at the crowing of the rooster, or in the morning. Mark 13:35

The exact day or hour we are not supposed to know. The general time frame we are supposed to know. Don't fall off to one side or the other. Dear reader, if you are focused too much on specific end-times details, you will miss God's command to get involved in revival and restoration. If, on the other hand, you have dismissed these prophecies as incomprehensible or irrelevant, you will miss vital revelatory information that you need to know to accomplish God's plans for believers.

The point is: Know what you need to know to be rightly involved in spiritual warfare in these endtimes. What God does reveal is for us to have and use. What He does not reveal is not for us to know.

Summary of Mark 13

To summarize the major points of Yeshua's teachings in Mark 13, we note:
1. There are necessary spiritual causes and effects in the end-times events.
2. Tribulation will increase in escalating stages.
   a. Tribulation is God's judgment on the world's evil system.

b. Tribulation is the attack of the world's system against the true believers in Yeshua.

3. Within the Church will be increasing levels of purging, purifying, intercession, evangelism, restoration, revival, and glory power.

4. The focus of end-times activities will be on God's plan to restore Israel and the devil's efforts to thwart that plan.

5. When the intensity of end-times events becomes too unbearable, Yeshua will intervene by His second coming.

6. At that time, God's people will be gathered up by the hands of angels.

7. The believers are to know enough of end-times prophecies to pray strategically and be prepared, but are not to be distracted by detailed time schemes.

Pray for Israel

As Israel is the focal point of God's plan for restoration and revival, it is imperative for true Christians everywhere to support Israel in prayer. As Israel is also the focal point of attack from the enemy, it is further imperative for the Church to pray for Israel's protection.

Pray for the peace of Jerusalem: "may they prosper who love you."   Psalm 122:6

Israel needs the intercessory prayer of believers. It is through that intercessory prayer for Israel that a special anointing of prosperity flows back to the Church.

Give and Take Between Jew and Gentile

Jewish believers in Yeshua play a unique role in interpreting and transmitting the revelations of end-times prophecy to the Church Body at large. There is a give-and-take relationship here.

145

The Jewish believers need to come to the Church at large to receive major revelations of spiritual life and salvation. (In fact it is the good things going on among Gentile Christians that attract the Jews to salvation in the first place. See Romans 11:11-14.)

But as the end-times revelations have so much to do with a restored remnant of Jewish or Israeli believers, they in turn will have a special perspective to understand those prophecies that the Gentile Church in general will not have. God has worked it out so that if we are to walk in the fullness of His plan for us, the Gentiles will have to receive from the Jews in certain areas, and the Jews will have to receive from the Gentiles in other areas.

It is both marvelous and humorous the way God is humbling us all to be able to bless us all the more in the end (Rom. 11:28-33). As the Church recognizes her Jewish roots of the past, her eyes will be opened to her Jewish restoration of the future. The fullness of blessing for the Jewish believers in Yeshua carries with it the fullness of blessing for all Gentile believers as well (Rom. 11:12,15-18).

How Is Israel Saved?

Not only will the recognition of her Jewish roots result in the fullness of the Church, but it will also result in the salvation of the Jewish people.

> *I do not desire, brethren, that you should be ignorant of this mystery, lest you should be wise in your own opinion, that blindness in part has happened to Israel until the fullness of the Gentiles has come in. And so all Israel will be saved.* Romans 11:25-26

As the Gentile Christians humble themselves and recognize their Jewish roots, the blindness on the Jews that keeps them from receiving Yeshua as Savior will be removed, and the Jews will be saved. In other words, the Church's recognition of her Jewish roots is what causes the Jews to be saved (among many other causes as well, of course).

"*And so all Israel will be saved.*" What is the "so" that makes all Israel get saved? The right attitude of the Church toward Israel. It's astounding. The fullness of blessing on the Gentiles attracts the Jews. The humility of the Gentiles to recognize their debt to the Jews removes the barriers in the spirit realm for the Jews to receive Christ. The restoring of the Jews to Yeshua as their Messiah ushers in the Second Coming and the fullness of God's Kingdom for everyone.

History bears out that when a nation with Gentile Christians accepts and embraces the Jews in a positive way, many Jewish people come to believe in Yeshua.

All Israel Saved

The spiritual warfare of the endtimes and the relationship between Jew and Gentile in the Church results in a massive turning of the Jewish people to Yeshua right before the Second Coming.

And so all Israel will be saved, as it is written: "The Deliverer will come out of Zion, and He will turn away ungodliness from Jacob." Romans 11:26

Here Paul is quoting from Isaiah to show that the endtimes culminate in a widespread Jewish revival. Peter quotes from Joel to demonstrate the same fact. Here is the rest of the verse from Joel that Peter quotes on Pentecost morning in Acts 2:21.

And it shall come to pass that whoever calls on the name of the LORD shall be saved. For in Mount Zion and in Jerusalem there shall be deliverance, as the LORD has said, among the remnant whom the LORD calls. Joel 2:32

Joel and Peter, and Isaiah and Paul are all prophesying the same fact: The end-times spiritual battle will give birth to a revival in Israel that will see many Jewish people saved. That end-times Jewish revival results in the second coming of Yeshua.

Note: Comparing Joel 2:32 to Romans 11:26 indicates that when Paul said that all Israel would be saved, he was referring to the remnant of Israelis that call upon the name of the Lord, as opposed to every person of Jewish blood. On the other hand, the indication is that the last-minute repentance and revival in Jerusalem will be of such magnitude that virtually every single person in the city will be saved.

The Gathering Point

Joel continues his account in chapter 3, setting the stage for the return of Christ.

For behold, in those days and at that time, when I bring back the captives of Judah and Jerusalem....   Joel 3:1

What is the general time frame for these end-times events? When God brings back the Jewish people to Judah and Jerusalem. That is what we are seeing take place in our own time. Many Jews have returned and many are yet to come.

When I bring back the captives of Judah and Jerusalem, I will also gather all nations, and bring them down to the Valley of Jehoshaphat; and I will enter into judgment with them there....   Joel 3:1-2

Here we have an excellent example of how God's restoration is matched with His judgment. God moves to restore the Jewish people by regathering them to Israel. Since the ungodly nations of the world hate God and hate Israel, this regathering becomes a focal point of their aggression. Therefore they begin to gather against Israel.

Israel, in a way, is acting as the bait in God's trap to draw the ungodly nations into judgment. What God meant for good to Israel turns into bad for the nations. It is their own antagonism and hatred that draw them into the trap of judgment. The very fact that they are there in the valley of battle proves that they are guilty and deserving of judgment.

This is the gathering of vultures which Yeshua said would be a sign of His imminent return (Luke 17:37).

Anti-Semitism and Anti-Zionism

What is the specific point of contention for which Yeshua is bringing the nations into judgment?

> *I will enter into judgment with them there on account of My people, My heritage Israel, whom they have scattered among the nations; they have also divided up My land.* Joel 3:2

This is a very specific and terrifying verse. The nations are being judged because of their negative treatment of the Jews. There are two accounts, one dealing with the scattering of the Jews, the other dealing with the dividing up of the land of Israel.

The scattering refers to the harsh treatment of the Jews during the last two thousand years when they were dispersed in Gentile nations. That harsh treatment includes such sordid history as: blood libels, desecration of the host libels, expulsions, persecutions, pogroms, crusades, inquisitions, the Holocaust, and so on. These crimes fall under the general title of anti-Semitism.

The dividing up of His land refers to the occupation of Israel by foreign nations over these centuries, but also to the partitioning of the land in modern times. It is the refusal to accept the right of the Jews to live autonomously in their own land. This opposition may be termed anti-Zionism.

It is this twofold crime, anti-Semitism and anti-Zionism, for which the nations will be held accountable to judgment. It is no wonder that the terrorist groups, Eastern religions, humanist movements, cult groups, secular media, and international political organizations are all unified on one point: their denunciation of Israel.

Stand by Israel

Believers, whatever you do, do not forsake Israel in these endtimes. No matter what you hear through the media's interpretation of the news, do not be deceived by their bias against Israel. There has been a misrepresentation of the facts, a purposeful demonic attempt to discredit Israel in the eyes of America and the world. But world opinion will pass away. It is God's Word that will stand.

Simply put, any nation that turns against Israel in the endtimes will come under judgment. Many people may not agree with that statement, but a survey of the entire Bible discloses hundreds of passages to support it.

Joel even makes special mention of the Philistines (which may be a veiled reference to the Palestinians as the word in Hebrew for Palestinian and Philistines is the same) and the Greeks (a possible veiled reference to Europe and Greek humanist philosophy in general) in their attempts to remove the Jews from their borders (vv. 4-6).

The Coming Armageddon

All this controversy over the Jews' right to live in the land of Israel causes tension to mount on the international political scene. This tension over Israel coincides with the spiritual warfare and signs and wonders mentioned in Chapter 2. International political tension over Israel will mount until all the nations of the world prepare for war against Israel.

Proclaim this among the nations: "Prepare for war!
Wake up the mighty men, let all the men of war draw

near, let them come up. Beat your plowshares into swords and your pruning hooks into spear...."

Joel 3:9-10

This is the buildup for the greatest clash the world has ever seen. The three themes of spiritual warfare, restoration of Israel, and judgment of the nations are all pending and at hand.

Assemble and come, all you nations... "Let the nations be wakened and come up to the Valley of Jehoshaphat; for there I will sit to judge all the surrounding nations." Multitudes, multitudes in the valley of decision! For the day of the LORD is near in the valley of decision.

Joel 3:11-12,14

Here come the nations to attack, all against Israel, in a world war of nuclear holocaust dimensions. This is what is known as the battle of Armageddon (*Har Meggido* in Hebrew). As the physical armies gather together, the spiritual armies gather together just above them.

Assemble and come, all you nations, and gather together all around. Cause Your mighty ones to go down there, O LORD. Joel 3:11

These mighty ones are the spiritual army of the Lord. It is made up of angels and saints. It may be at this time that the angels go forth to gather the elect from the four winds—either to be protected from this battle or to join in it on the Lord's side. To what extent the army will include believers who have previously died is not stated.

The Spiritual Army of the Air

Zechariah and Isaiah also make reference to a supernatural army that comes in the air at the Second Coming.

Thus the LORD my God will come, and all the saints
with You.   Zechariah 14:5

The word *saints* could be translated also as "holy ones." It is
from the same root word (*kadosh*) as "sanctified ones" in the following verse from Isaiah.

I have commanded My sanctified ones; I have also
called My mighty ones for My anger.   Isaiah 13:3

Isaiah 13 describes the fall of Babylon in a way parallel to
Revelation 18. Both describe a sudden collapse of the power of
Babylon right at the time of the coming of the Lord. The word for
"mighty ones" is the same as the root word (*gibor*) for "mighty
ones" in Joel 3. So Isaiah 13, Joel 3, and Zechariah 14 are all
speaking of the last moment of battle on the terrible Day of the
Lord; all three speak of an army of mighty holy ones gathered together in a supernatural manner.

The LORD of hosts musters the army for battle. They
come from a far country, from the end of heaven—the
LORD and His [vessels] *of indignation, to destroy the*
whole land.   Isaiah 13:4-5

It is astonishing how parallel these three passages are. It is
possible that the believers will be so caught up in spiritual intercession and warfare that as this ultimate war breaks out, they will be
swept into the air and translated supernaturally to take part in the
actual battle itself. Obviously conditions would have to reach quite
a state of tension, and the prayer level of God's people reach quite a
state of intensity, for such a phenomenon to take place. But it is certainly within the grasp of faith and within the guidelines of prophetic Scriptures.

When we compare this movement of a spiritual army with
Yeshua's statement in Mark 13:27 that at His coming His angels

would gather the elect from the four winds, we have a very consistent picture.

The Grapes of Wrath

All these factors bring the spiritual controversy on planet Earth to such a climax that it cannot be reconciled in any other manner than the direct intervention of the Lord.

Put in the sickle, for the harvest is ripe. Come, go down; for the winepress is full, the vats overflow—for their wickedness is great. Joel 3:13

Another angel came out from the altar, who had power over fire, and he cried with a loud voice to him who had the sharp sickle, saying, "Thrust in your sharp sickle and gather the clusters of the vine of the earth, for her grapes are fully ripe." Revelation 14:18

Human history and human iniquity have hit their bursting point. There is no room left for God to hold back His anger. The grapes of wrath are the people of earth who are so ripe with sin they are ready to burst. The winepress is this last battle where blood will flow like wine for miles around.

The Moment of Darkness

Here even the sun will darken because of the horror of the moment, just as it did at the time of the crucifixion. There are certain things the sun cannot bear to see.

The sun and moon will grow dark, and the stars will diminish their brightness. Joel 3:15

Isaiah describes the same moment of wrath.

Behold, the day of the LORD comes, cruel, with both wrath and fierce anger, to lay the land desolate; and He will destroy its sinners from it. For the stars of heaven

*and their constellations will not give their light; the sun
will be darkened in its going forth, and the moon will
not cause its light to shine.*   Isaiah 13:9-10

This is the same time of darkness stated in Joel 2 and Acts 2.
The culmination of the spiritual warfare is this mighty battle on
the physical plane. The signs and wonders of glory have resulted
in the final judgment of darkness to the world.

While this moment is horrible, it is also a venting of the pent-
up anger of the Lord against evil. Joy and freedom result from the
final release of God's justice.

We recall that in Luke 12 Yeshua said He had a fire to throw
upon the earth and that He desired greatly for it to happen. This
fire was both the fire of glory and power for the believers and the
fire of judgment and wrath upon the world.

When President Truman unleashed the atomic bomb on
Japan, there was great regret at the loss of human life, and yet
there was great relief that the destruction would bring an end to
the war.

The Nuclear Fire

So it is that the fire unleashed at the return of the Lord will
consume the wicked in a horrible annihilation. The spiritual fire of
the Lord will be manifest outwardly to the ungodly as a nuclear
holocaust.

*This shall be the plague with which the LORD will
strike all the people who fought against Jerusalem:
their flesh shall dissolve while they stand on their feet,
their eyes shall dissolve in their sockets, and their
tongues shall dissolve in their mouths.* Zechariah 14:12

*Behold, the day is coming, burning like an oven, and all
the proud, yes, all who do wickedly will be stubble. And
the day which is coming shall burn them up.* Malachi 4:1

The day of the Lord will come as a thief in the night, in which the heavens will pass away with a great noise, and the elements will melt with fervent heat; both the earth and the works that are in it will be burned up.

2 Peter 3:10

In a certain sense, it is the human race that brings its own history to a close. As nuclear weapons are released at the final war of Armageddon, the end of the human race will come. Yeshua will have no choice but to intervene.

Multitudes on the face of the earth will be engulfed in fire. As the nuclear flames spread across the earth, God's Spirit will move at the same time to protect His people. For those who have been receptive to the Holy Spirit, His presence will reach them shortly before the nuclear flames. They will be transformed into a glorious state in a moment and swept into the air unharmed and unsinged.

The ungodly, or those who have resisted the Holy Spirit, will find themselves engulfed and destroyed by the very flames they have started. There will be no legal or spiritual grounds for the Holy Spirit to protect such people. God's judgment upon them is simply to give them over to the results of their own actions. They will reap the fruit they have sown. Their hatred and vehemence will be turned on their own heads. Their flesh will dissolve as the force waves of the nuclear blasts hit them.

The Landing

Because Yeshua cannot allow all His elect people on earth to be destroyed, He will cut short the time and intervene at the last possible moment. One more moment and all flesh would be destroyed.

The LORD also will roar from Zion; and utter His voice from Jerusalem; the heavens and earth will shake; but

155

the LORD will be a shelter for His people, and the
strength of the children of Israel. Joel 3:16

The Lord's intervention is to protect His people on earth. He has promised to defend Israel. When they can defend themselves no longer, He puts an end to human history as we know it.

I will gather all the nations to battle against Jerusalem;
the city shall be taken, the houses rifled, and the women
ravished. Half of the city shall go into captivity, but the
remnant of the people shall not be cut off from the city.
Zechariah 14:2

As the nations close in on Jerusalem, the Lord will break forth with a mighty roar. Just as the Jews perceive they are losing the war, they cry out in desperation to Yeshua to save them. His answer will be instantaneous and awesome.

The LORD will go forth and fight against those nations,
as He fights in the day of battle. Zechariah 14:3

Yeshua comes back as the conquering King of Israel. He comes back in a lightning-like military invasion at the head of the armies of the Lord. His immediate point of invasion will be to defend Jerusalem from the military attack of the nations.

And in that day His feet will stand on the Mount of
Olives, which faces Jerusalem on the east. And the
Mount of Olives shall be split in two from east to west.
Zechariah 14:4

Yeshua will land like an Israeli paratrooper, hitting the very target with His feet from which He lifted off almost two thousand years ago. In a similar manner to which He left, He will come back.

Intervening Army

John also saw Yeshua returning at the head of a large army.

Now I saw heaven opened, and behold, a white horse.
And He who sat on him was called Faithful and True,
and in righteousness He judges and makes war. And the
armies in heaven, clothed in fine linen, white and clean,
followed Him on white horses.   Revelation 19:11,14

Yeshua intervenes with His saintly army at the last possible moment. All the nations have gathered against Israel; the tide of war has turned decisively against Israel, and Jerusalem begins to fall. Those in Jerusalem turn in desperation to Yeshua to rescue them. The believers in Jerusalem are interceding, as well as Christians around the world.

The two war patterns of the endtimes, first the removal of the northern army and then the gathered battle of Armageddon, have a certain parallel to the 1967 Six-day War and the 1973 Yom Kippur War in Israel. In 1967, the Israelis launched a brilliant air strike followed by a successful tank attack. In only six days, they won the war, captured much territory, and took back Jerusalem.

In the intervening years, the Arab nations looked for revenge and continually built up their arms for another war. When they attacked, the Israeli defense forces were caught off guard. The Yom Kippur War was launched by the Arab armies on the most sacred day of the Jewish calendar, right on the biblical feast of *Yom Kippur* itself.

For the first time in her brief history, Israel actually began to lose the war. These were desperate and tragic moments. Israel came close to being obliterated that day. After tremendous losses, and with the aid of an emergency air lift from America ordered by President Richard Nixon, the war was finally turned around, and Israel survived. The armed forces of both America and Russia were put on red alert. While many did not know it, the world tottered on the brink of international disaster.

The Day of Atonement

The Yom Kippur War had a deep, sobering effect on the Israelis, causing a period of psychological reevaluation that shook the government and changed the face of Israeli politics. It is interesting to note that this war broke out on a day designated in the Bible for repentance and atonement.

> *It shall be in that day that I will seek to destroy all the nations that come against Jerusalem. And I will pour on the house of David and on the inhabitants of Jerusalem the Spirit of grace and of supplication; then they will look upon Me whom they have pierced. Yes, they will mourn for Him as one mourns for his only son, and grieve for Him as one grieves for a firstborn.*
>
> Zechariah 12:9-10

In the very midst of war and the shedding of blood, a turning of heart results in spiritual revelation for the nation.

In the first century, the major spring festivals were all prophetically fulfilled in one year. The Passover was fulfilled in Yeshua's crucifixion, the Firstfruits festival (Lev. 23:10) in Yeshua's resurrection, and the Feast of Weeks in the outpouring of the Holy Spirit at Pentecost. So too, many of the end-times prophecies concerning the second coming of Yeshua will be fulfilled in one sweep at the autumn biblical feasts of Trumpets, the Day of Atonement, and the Feast of Tabernacles.

These holy days cover a period of two to three weeks, which is more than enough for such world-shaking events to take place.

Worship and the Rapture

The spiritual pressure of those days will be almost unbearable. The people of God will be in such a state of constant intercession that signs and wonders, previously unheard of, will take place all over the world. Angels will make an appearance on the scene. Open visions of heaven and the throne room of God will be regular experiences in prayer meetings.

The true Body of Messiah on earth at that time will be engaged in a continuing "upper room" experience. The worship of the saints will be so concentrated that they will feel themselves virtually lifted into heaven. Whether in their physical bodies or out, they will hardly know the difference (2 Cor. 12:2-3).

Worship will become so powerful that it will be a mere step away from being lifted into the air physically to meet Yeshua.

As Yeshua was able to be lifted into the air in His resurrection body, so will it be when we are changed into our immortal bodies in the twinkling of an eye (1 Cor. 15:52).

I saw something like a sea of glass mingled with fire, and those who have the victory over the beast...standing on the sea of glass, having harps of God. They sing the song of Moses, the servant of God, and the song of the Lamb....behold, the temple of the tabernacle of the testimony in heaven was opened. Revelation 15:2-3,5

The increasingly miraculous level of worship in the endtimes brings the saints of God into a place of spiritual victory, releases the power of God on earth, and prepares the people of God to be caught up in the air at the coming of Yeshua.

Transforming Fire

As worship causes a lifting up of the saints, intercession causes a release of the fire of God. The intercession of Acts 1 brought the falling of fire in Acts 2. The same power that transformed the saints into super "aliveness" also resulted in death to those who lied and stole in their midst (Acts 5). Power is power. The power that lights a light bulb can also electrocute. Fire fell on the disciples at Pentecost, but it also fell on the soldiers who tried to capture Elijah and killed them (2 Kings 1).

As the disciples interceded in the first century, the fire of God fell. As the disciples of the Last Days intercede, the fire will fall in a greater way. The fire in the first century transformed the believers on the inside. The end-times fire will not only do that, but it will also transform all flesh. Flesh that has not been sealed by the Holy Spirit will dissolve and melt. Flesh that has a pure spirit will be transfigured into a higher, deathless state of being.

> *Flesh and blood cannot inherit the kingdom of God.... Behold, I tell you a mystery: We shall not all sleep, but we shall be changed—in a moment, in the twinkling of an eye, at the last trumpet. For the trumpet will sound, and the dead will be raised incorruptible, and we shall all be changed.* 1 Corinthians 15:50-52

Normal bodies cannot handle the full power of God. They have to be transformed. The fire power of God will transform them. The power is God's glory. God's glory going into the bodies will make the bodies glorified (glory-fied). Those glorified bodies can be lifted into the air as Yeshua's glorified body was. The moment they are glorified is the moment they will be swept into the air to meet Yeshua.

The Closing Moments

At the closing moments of Armageddon, the saints are interceding with fiery intensity. The armies of the nations are on the verge of conquering Jerusalem. The fire of God falls. Nuclear weapons may be deployed. The Jews in Jerusalem cry out to

Yeshua to rescue them, saying, *"Blessed is He who comes in the name of the Lord."*

The last trumpet blows. The fire of God spreads on earth. The nations that attacked Jerusalem are destroyed. All flesh melts. The bodies of the saints who have died are resurrected. The bodies of the saints who are alive are transfigured into glorified bodies. The resurrection of the dead saints and the glorifying of the bodies of the living saints takes place nearly at the same time.

Yeshua descends with His heavenly brigades. The resurrected saints and the glorified saints are swept into the air to meet Him. The earth itself is physically altered. The war is terminated. The cleanup operation begins. A new era of peace and prosperity begins.

> *Everyone who is left of all the nations which came against Jerusalem shall go up from year to year to worship the King, the LORD of hosts, and to keep the Feast of Tabernacles.* Zechariah 14:16

The inaugural celebration of this new millennium will be the biblical Feast of Tabernacles. People from all nations will celebrate this feast every year. The Feast of Tabernacles is also referred to as the Feast of Ingathering (Exod. 23:16). It celebrates the last great harvest of the ingathering of God's Kingdom. The end of this age will mark the dawn of a new one.

CHAPTER 6

THE MILLENNIUM

by Keith Intrater

Period of Restoration

The purpose of the new messianic age is to restore the quality of life on the earth that God originally intended. He created us to live in a paradise. We ruined that paradise through our sin and by allowing satan to take advantage of us.

God's plan of salvation ultimately leads to a restoration of that paradise. God did not make a mistake when He placed us in the Garden of Eden. The fact that we got off the correct track does not alter God's original intention.

God does not change. He was right and always will be right. As we repent and come back to Him, we are conformed more and more to His original design for us. What we were before we fell foreshadows what we will be when our restoration is completed. Then we will go on from there. Our origins foreshadow our destiny.

The death and resurrection of Yeshua provided the means for the human race to be restored to God's design for us. The Body of people who believe in Yeshua is where the process of restoration primarily takes place.

That [God] *may send Jesus Christ, who was preached to you before, whom heaven must receive until the times of*

restoration of all things, which God has spoken by the
mouth of all His holy prophets since the world began.

Acts 3:20-21

Yeshua is in Heaven now, and we are moving ever closer to the restoration of all things. To restore means to bring back to a condition that already existed. To restore all things means that nothing of the good things of Eden will be missing.

When God made us in Eden, He described us and all of creation as "very good." From the fall of Adam and Eve, all the prophets throughout history have been calling us to come back to God and to those very good conditions.

The Breaking of the Vessel

Life as God created it was a work of art, a masterpiece of beauty. The Garden of Eden could be likened to a fine piece of ceramic pottery. Our sin fractured that life of beauty and perfection.

This is the parable that God told Jeremiah to enact before the people of Jerusalem to demonstrate the repercussions of their sins.

Go and get a potter's earthen flask, and take some of the
elders of the people and of the priests. Then you shall
break the flask in the sight of the men who go with you.

Jeremiah 19:1,10

The fracturing of the vessel symbolizes the destruction caused by sin. Jewish mystical tradition sees all of history under the general theme called *Shevirat Ha Kelim* and *Tikkun*. *Shevirat Ha Kelim* means "the breaking of the vessels." *Tikkun* means "restoration or the repairing" of those vessels.

The destruction of Jerusalem and the dispersing of the Jewish people is seen as a breaking of the vessel. The reestablishment of Israel as a nation is seen as a repairing of the vessel. Likewise, we may see the fall of Adam as the first great fracture and the Kingdom of God (or the new creation) as the great restoration.

All of life falls under one of these two categories. As we co-operate with the law of sin and death, we cause destruction and fracturing. As we cooperate with God's law of the Spirit of life, we move forward into restoration (Rom. 8:2). Every action, small or large, either destroys life or restores it.

It is as if God is faced with a cosmic "Humpty-Dumpty" problem in dealing with the human race. We were in a high place. We fell and broke to pieces. How can God put us back together? Actually He has to recreate us spiritually and start over from the inside out.

The Elijah Ministry

A prophetic ministry of restoration must take place before Yeshua comes back.

> *And His disciples asked Him, saying, "Why then do the scribes say that Elijah must come first?" Jesus answered and said to them, "Indeed, Elijah is coming first and will restore all things. But I say to you that Elijah has come already, and they did not know him but did to him whatever they wished."*   Matthew 17:10-12

The disciples are asking Yeshua about the generally accepted viewpoint of the times that Elijah would introduce the Messiah. Yeshua answers that the Elijah ministry does come first. Yeshua explains that the purpose of the Elijah ministry is to restore all things. In other words, the reason an Elijah ministry must precede the coming of the Messiah is that there must be a restoration of all things. The ministry of restoration must occur before Yeshua fulfills His ultimate role as the Messiah-King.

This dialogue took place after John the Baptist was behead-ed. Yeshua states that John partially fulfilled the Elijah role in the sense that he did introduce Yeshua. John did not complete the full mission. John did preach a type of restoration message when he challenged society to return to the commandments of the Law. He challenged people on economic injustice. He challenged soldiers and tax collectors on graft and repression, and politicians on immorality (Luke 3:7-19).

Demanding society to conform to biblical moral absolutes is part of the Elijah ministry of the endtimes, and must take place before Yeshua returns. Before that message can be preached to society, a balanced perspective on the role of biblical Law must be understood within the Church at large.

End-Times Elijah

When Yeshua said that John was Elijah, He did not mean there was some sort of reincarnation, but simply that John fulfilled a similar prophetic function as Elijah, and that John operated under a similar anointing. So when Yeshua says that Elijah will come, He does not necessarily mean that Elijah will come personally, but that a ministry and anointing parallel to Elijah's role must take place.

Yeshua said that Elijah had come already. That referred to John the Baptist. But Yeshua also said that in addition to John's ministry, Elijah will yet come in the future with a ministry to restore all things. Some see this end-times Elijah as Elijah himself, others a contemporary prophet, and others as a widespread movement of moral, spiritual, and social restoration in the Church as a whole.

In any case, the point is that a ministry that brings biblical order within the Church and challenges society to adhere to biblical morality occurs before the return of Yeshua.

The purpose of the messianic or millennial Kingdom is to restore the earth back toward the living conditions of Eden. The ministry of the Body of believers in the endtimes is to restore biblical values on earth as much as possible before Yeshua comes back. We prepare the way for the coming of the great King.

Authority Restored

God's design for mankind at the time of creation was correct. It still is correct. God's way will win out. He is eternal. No matter how long it takes us to get in line with His plan, He is not the one who will have to change. It will be His way or no way at all.

God designed us to live in perfect harmony with Him. The physical creation was a perfect place for us to live. We are spiritual beings living in earthen bodies designed for the conditions of this planet. We were created in God's image. God is spirit, and we were to be His spiritual children living in "earth suits" in this physical environment. We were made in His likeness to be like Him, as children are like their parents.

God gave us a great commandment to take dominion and rule over this earth. We were to exercise authority under God to govern the earth in a benevolent way.

When we sinned, we fell from that position of godly dominion and yielded our authority to satan, who became the god of this world by our default. Yeshua came in the position of a descendant of Adam, broke the power of the devil, and regained authority on this planet on behalf of the human race. Yeshua spoiled the devil. He spoiled him of the authority that the devil had usurped from the human race at the time of the fall.

Now Yeshua is offering that authority back to the human race to anyone who will accept Him as their Lord and authority. To accept Yeshua as the authority in your life is to accept as well authority through Him over this planet. His authority to you is also His authority through you. If we are people under authority, then we are also people of authority.

The Great Commission

After Yeshua was raised from the dead, He gave us a commandment to preach and exercise spiritual authority in His name. This Great Commission is parallel to the great commandment of dominion that God gave us in the first place. God called it dominion in Genesis 1, and Yeshua called it authority in Matthew 28. But dominion and authority are virtually the same thing. Yeshua is referred to as the last Adam.

It is as if Yeshua were saying, "Look, people, God told you to do something. You didn't do it. Because you didn't do it, you inflicted great harm on yourselves. Now I've fixed you up and given you a second chance. Let's see if we can get it right this time. The game plan is this: Go out and take dominion. Let's try it again."

God created us to be like Him. Since we ruined ourselves, He had to recreate us in Yeshua. God commissioned us to act like Him in dominion and authority. Since we defaulted on that authority, He has to recommission us in Yeshua.

When we sin, we disqualify ourselves from spiritual authority. When we make religious excuses for not exercising spiritual authority, we avoid using what is available to us.

Heaven on Earth

God designed us to be His representatives on this planet. He created us to live on the earth. Generally speaking, God's primary purpose is not for us to go to Heaven, but for us to live in cooperation with Heaven here.

Then I, John, saw the holy city, New Jerusalem, coming down out of heaven from God.　　　Revelation 21:2

New Jerusalem is coming down out of Heaven here to the earth.

And he...showed me the great city, the holy Jerusalem, descending out of heaven from God.　　Revelation 21:10

The idea is not so much for us to get out of this place and go to Heaven as it is for Heaven to come down here to reestablish a heavenly living environment on earth. Yeshua's prayer was not for us to be taken to Heaven, but for God's will as it occurs in Heaven to be brought down and reproduced on earth.

Reclaiming This Planet

We were made to live on earth. It is our goal to reclaim this planet for the Kingdom of God. This is a different sense of direction from what many believers have. We are not trying to escape so much as we are believing to recapture.

In the Garden of Eden we lived in ideal conditions on this planet. We had an ideal relationship with God. He walked and talked with us. The kingdoms of this world are to become kingdoms of our Lord (Rev. 11:15). We have Heaven in our hearts but want to see those heavenly realities reinstated on this planet.

Your kingdom come. Your will be done on earth as it is in heaven.   Matthew 6:10

We are praying and working for God's Kingdom to come down and be established here. The Kingdom of God exists wherever the will of God is done. Things on this earth are not being done according to God's will. Things are not being done as they are in Heaven. We are out to change that.

When we change something to the will of God, we have introduced the Kingdom of God to a certain extent. We are out to make every aspect of life on earth patterned after life as it is in Heaven. We want to impose a heavenly lifestyle here. We are looking for Heaven to come to earth. The Kingdom of God may be described as "Heaven on earth."

The Kingdom Within You

The place that Heaven starts is on the inside of us. When we are spiritually reborn, our innermost being is changed from darkness to light. On the inside we are taken out of the kingdom of satan and transferred into the Kingdom of God (Col. 1:13).

The Kingdom of God starts from the inside out. We aim to change everything on this planet that is contrary to the will of God. The first area we have to change is our own thought life and attitudes.

> *Do not be conformed to this world, but be transformed by the renewing of your mind, that you may prove what is that good and acceptable and perfect will of God.*
>
> Romans 12:2

We have various thoughts that run contrary to the will of God. Every time we take control over one of those thoughts and turn it around in the right direction, we have extended the realm of the Kingdom of God on earth one more degree. Each time you renew your mind to the will of God, you are actually advancing the Kingdom of God and bringing Heaven into the sphere of this earth.

Each thought that is taken captive is one small step in ushering in the millennial reign of Messiah Yeshua.

The Expanding Kingdom

The Kingdom of God expands from the inside out. It starts with righteousness and peace and joy in the inner man. The Kingdom of God is within you. But from within you it grows like a seed to affect every area of your life and eventually the world around you (Rom. 14:17, Luke 17:21, Mark 4:31).

When we submit our spirit to God's will, we are reborn. When we submit our minds to God's will, our minds are renewed. God's Kingdom brings life to any area that is submitted to God's will. That is why obedience causes blessing. God's will is to bless us. Obedience is to submit to God's will. So obedience is to submit to God's blessing.

God's salvation brings restoration to every area of life. Salvation to the spirit is rebirth. Salvation to the body is healing. Salvation to one's finances is provision and prosperity. Salvation to a community brings revival. Salvation to the international community brings an end to war and famine and restores Israel to a place of leadership among the nations.

Just as healing is part of God's overall plan of salvation for the physical body, so is Zionism, or the restoration of Israel, a part of God's overall plan of salvation for the international political scene.

Any area of life that is submitted to God's will and receives restoration manifests the Kingdom of God on earth. In this way, every act of obedience and submission that we do helps to bring forth the Kingdom of God.

The Millennium

The Bible describes a period of a thousand years in which the devil's influence over humanity is halted and a spiritual form of government, led by the most dedicated followers of Yeshua, rules over the nations of the earth.

Then I saw an angel coming down from heaven, having the key to the bottomless pit and a great chain in his hand. He laid hold of the dragon, that serpent of old, who is the Devil and Satan, and bound him for a thousand years; and he cast him into the bottomless pit, and shut him up, and set a seal on him, so that he should deceive the nations no more till the thousand years were finished. But after these things he must be released for a little while.   Revelation 20:1-3

This period of a thousand years is often referred to as the Millennium, which simply comes from the Latin word *mille*, meaning one thousand.

Ruling Now

Some people refer to the Millennium as the period in which we are now living. This viewpoint, called "present-" or "amillennial," has some important truth in it. It is true that at the resurrection of Jesus the devil was bound, and believers were given authority over the devil. It is also true that in a spiritual sense believers are ruling and reigning in this life through the righteousness we have by faith (Rom. 5:17).

Just as satan's position was lowered at the time of the fall of Adam, so it was lowered again in the ministry of Yeshua and His disciples (Luke 10:17-19). Then at the cross, the satanic power and principality over this world was broken once and for all (Col. 2:15, John 12:31). The new authority that Yeshua won on behalf of the human race was delegated to the Body of believers at the Great Commission (Matt. 28, Mark 16).

So in a very real way satan has been bound, and we are reigning with Yeshua now. The one-thousand-year period can be seen as a symbolic number referring to the extended time of the church age in which we are living. In addition, a strong parallel can be made between the events surrounding the first-century destruction of Israel by Rome and the prophecies about the endtimes in the New Testament.

Present Millennialism

This view that the Millennium is going on at the present time has the benefit of motivating believers to exercise their full spiritual authority now, without making excuses about being in a wrong time period. So in a practical way this viewpoint encourages people to live out the fullest degree of their Christian activity and experience.

So present millennialism emphasizes the following major points:

1. Satan is bound now.
2. Believers should exercise their spiritual authority.
3. Bible prophecies can be identified with the climactic events of the first century.
4. Highly symbolic language can be taken in a figurative application.
5. Believers are motivated to get involved without limitations.

On the other hand, the signs and judgments described in Revelation 6-19 have a worldwide dimension and a finality to them that goes beyond the events of the first century. The seals and trumpets and bowls could not have been fully completed as the greatest disasters of mankind when events like the Holocaust were yet to take place.

As we explained earlier, the events of the first century have a certain similarity to those of the Last Days. The events of the first century serve as a pattern and a parallel, but they are not the ultimate fulfillment of the Last Days prophecies. Because of the similarity of events, it is understandable how some would see them as the fulfillment.

In addition, the large war of confrontation between the armies of Heaven and the nations of earth that is described in Revelation 19:11-21 immediately precedes the binding of satan and his banishment to the bottomless pit. The judgment of the nations, the destruction of the beast, and the international conflict are all of a proportion that does not match the destruction of Jerusalem in 70 A.D.

What we see rather is the culmination of a series of climactic events on a worldwide scale that has similarities to previous history but is even more horrible, and which is about to take place before us. With the Jews back in Jerusalem, the nations arraying themselves according to prophecy, and the upheavals taking place around the world, we see the stage being set for the full impact of what is described in the Book of Revelation.

The Resurrected Saints

Revelation 20 describes a special group of believers who are raised from the dead and given a role of leadership during the millennial period.

I saw the souls of those who had been beheaded for their witness to Jesus and for the word of God, who had not worshiped the beast or his image, and had not received his mark on their foreheads or on their hands. And they lived and reigned with Christ for a thousand years. But the rest of the dead did not live again until the thousand years were finished. This is the first resurrection. Revelation 20:4-5

Those who are raised up for ruling and reigning in the Millennium are those who have witnessed for the gospel, resisted the world system of evil, and been killed for their faith. This martyrdom may be literal, or it may refer to those who have given their life totally for the gospel.

In order for these people to be present, there must have been a time previous to the start of the Millennium in which their witnessing went forth and they were persecuted. Since that is still happening, and since we are still under attack from a world system of evil, we can see that we are in the period leading up to the Millennium. There must also be a time, referred to as the first resurrection, when this group of people, who have already been witnessing for the gospel, are raised up.

Different Types of People

The passage is also clear that resurrected saints of the first resurrection are a special group of people. They are the ones who will rule and reign. There are also the unbelievers who will not be judged until the second resurrection. Thirdly, there are the believers who were not part of the first resurrection, who will be raised up at the White Throne of Judgment (v. 12). Finally, there are those people, both believers and unbelievers, who are alive on the earth during the Millennium, over whom the special class of saints is ruling.

The saints who are ruling during the thousand years will have been raised from the dead, so they will be living in their resurrection bodies. Since it is the resurrected saints who are ruling, the general population of that time will not have resurrection bodies. The resurrected saints will rule over the general non-resurrected population.

The general population will live long and healthy lives since the demonic ruling forces will have been bound, but they will ultimately be subjected to death since they do not have resurrection bodies (Isa. 65:17). The resurrected saints will interact with the people as Yeshua did after His resurrection (Luke 24, John 20), and even as the group of Old Testament saints did who entered Jerusalem after the resurrection of Yeshua (Matt.27:53). The interaction of the resurrected Yeshua with the believers in Jerusalem may be seen as a foretaste of the interaction of people in the Millennium.

The Last Battle

So life goes on in a wonderful way for a thousand years during the millennial reign. After that time the devil is released for a short period to gather together all those who are still against God for one final attack.

> *Now when the thousand years have expired, Satan will be released from his prison and will go out to deceive the nations which are on the four corners of the earth, Gog and Magog, to gather them together to battle,*

whose number is as the sand of the sea. They went up on the breadth of the earth and surrounded the camp of the saints and the beloved city. And fire came down from God out of heaven and devoured them.

Revelation 20:7-9

Notice that this battle is similar to the battle described in chapter 19 at the beginning of the Millennium. An overview of the Scriptures would show that there are three battles described in end-times prophecy. The first, described in Joel 2:20, has the forces of the northern army driven back away from the land of Israel.

The second battle, described in Ezekiel 38-39, Zechariah 14, and Revelation 19, comes not too long after that as a massive retaliation by the forces of evil against Israel. This time Israel begins to lose, and Yeshua is forced to intervene. That intervention inaugurates the Millennium.

The third battle, here in Revelation 20, involves a final attack which is summarily consumed by fire in a direct act of God.

The Last Release

It is interesting to note that satan is released for a time. This temporary release is by determined counsel of God and serves a purpose. Satan immediately goes to gather the ungodly for an attack. It is clear, therefore, that even at the end of the Millennium, a large group of people around the world are still in rebellion against God. They have not had opportunity to manifest that rebellion until this time.

That last attack is the last of the last opportunities for anyone to attack the Lord. Judgment at that time is absolute. ("*He who often rebuked, and hardens his neck, will suddenly be destroyed, and that without remedy*"—Prov. 29:1.) The people on earth during the Millennium still have the free-will option to turn their hearts away from God. Even with the devil imprisoned and the government of righteous people on earth, many still choose to go the wrong way.

Why the Last Release?

The immediate purpose of the release of satan is to draw together the evil-hearted people so their real colors will be exposed, manifested, and judged. (You would think that after one thousand years of imprisonment, satan would have changed his heart, but that is obviously not so. He is evil to the core and only grows more embittered with time.)

If satan is released at that time to exercise his own will briefly, it is logical that the rest of the imprisoned demonic hordes will be released as well. The people in the Millennium are given their right to act on their own free will right through to the very end. God gives people time to exercise their own free will and thereby choose their own destiny. God then brings to light the intentions of their hearts and judges them accordingly.

The Final Judgment

At this final release of satan, all the demons of hell, all the saints on earth, and any ungodly people left are given their last opportunity to take sides. It may even be that the men and women who had been imprisoned in hell are given release along with satan at this time. By this late event, all the workings of godliness and ungodliness will have been made so plain that all evil will be completely without excuse. After thousands of years of warning, example, forgiveness, and punishment, the ultimate judgment comes.

Then I saw a great white throne and Him who sat on it....I saw the dead, small and great, standing before God, and books were opened. And another book was opened, which is the Book of Life. And the dead were

177

judged according to their works, by the things which
were written in the books.   Revelation 20:11-12

At this judgment there are two kinds of books: of life and of
death. This shows that many of those who are appointed for eternal life receive that verdict here and not at the beginning of the
Millennium.

Satan has been released briefly to make all judgment manifest. The saints of God will be in accord with that difficult decision, as God cooperates with us to bind and loose on earth (Matt.
18:18). It is a corporate decision of God and His earthly family to
allow one last period of release so that all good and evil will have
its last chance to sort itself out.

The Lake of Fire

The devil will be taken and thrown into the lake of fire for
eternal punishment. This is not hell but a worse place. Hell is a
prison presided over by demonic spirits where dead people are. At
this time of the end, the people held by death and hell will be released for judgment, then the demonic chieftains named Death and
Hades will be thrown with satan into the lake of fire.

The devil, who deceived them, was cast into the lake of
fire and brimstone where the beast and the false prophet
are. And they will be tormented day and night forever
and ever. The sea gave up the dead who were in it, and
Death and Hades delivered up the dead who were in
them....Then Death and Hades were cast into the lake of
fire....And anyone not found written in the Book of Life
was cast into the lake of fire.   Revelation 20:10,13-15

The demonic ruler called Death is not thrown into the fire
until the end of the Millennium. Death is the last enemy to be defeated (1 Cor. 15). Death lost much of its power when Yeshua was

raised from the dead. It lost even more power at the start of the Millennium. But since it is not fully destroyed until the end of the Millennium, death has a limited influence throughout the millennial period. People will live much longer, but some will die. Satan, Death, and Hades were angels originally created by God. They rebelled against God and God's children. Satan is the highest evil angel, and Death (the evil angel who presides over death) and Hades (the evil angel who presides over hell) are two of the next highest leaders.

The Story of the Millennium

To summarize, the endtimes are filled with upheaval and turmoil. At a great battle, Yeshua intervenes with His own armies. The devil is bound in chains and incarcerated for a thousand years but is not fully destroyed. Many people left on the face of the earth, at different levels of faith, pass into the new era. Saints who have been particularly dedicated to the Lord live on earth in resurrection bodies. All the rest of the people who have died previously, both good and bad, have to wait until the final resurrection.

The resurrected believers run a new godly kind of society that is generally free from sickness, death, and demonic influence. People begin to live longer but some still die. The world is in process of being restored to an Eden-like state. Prosperity, peace, and true worship are spreading over the planet. The people living still exercise their own free will and some turn their hearts away.

At the end of the thousand years, all the satanic forces are released to gather the ungodly people for one last attack against God. The attack is summarily destroyed. The final judgment comes. The fallen angels and the human beings who have persisted in their rebellion are thrown permanently into a tormenting fire.

A New Start

Now God and His family, the purified remnant of the human race, are ready to set forth in a paradise existence called the new heavens and new earth. All people now have deathless resurrection bodies. Evil is purged. God and man, Heaven and earth, are re-united. Life in the universe finally is allowed to get started the way God designed it to be. The ultimate restoration to a similar state as the Garden of Eden is effected.

At the start of the new heavens and new earth, heavenly Jerusalem descends out of the sky to be reunited with earth. In a certain sense, this is the opposite of the withdrawal and separation that occurred between Heaven and earth at the time of the fall. We have come full cycle. The Great White Throne Judgment is the complement of the judgment and curse of the fall.

The Two Floods

A figurative parallel exists as well between the flood of Noah, which took place roughly a thousand years after the fall, and the events that take place at the start of the Millennium, one thousand years before the final judgment.

> *"Where is the promise of His coming?"...by the word of God the heavens were of old, and the earth standing out of water and in the water, by which the world that then existed perished, being flooded with water. But the heavens and the earth which are now preserved by the same word, are reserved for fire until the day of judgment...Do not forget...that with the Lord one day is as a thousand years, and a thousand years as one day.* 2 Peter 3:4-8

"What happened to all those prophecies concerning the end-times?" Peter asks rhetorically. He says the Second Coming will be parallel to the flood of Noah, but this time with fire instead of water. After the flood a new age and a new start dawned under the rainbow covenant of peace.

The Millennium will be the start of a new era of messianic peace. The earth was cataclysmically different after the flood of Noah, and yet it was still the same planet. A different relationship existed between God and man, but men were men. So in the Millennium, everything will be radically transformed, yet it will still be planet Earth, and the inhabitants will still be people.

Geological Changes

There is evidence of enormous geological changes in the crust of the earth. Rationalist scientists say this must have taken place over billions of years. The evidence fits better, however, into a model in which a sudden cataclysm several thousand years ago drastically affected rock formations, vegetation, animal life, and even mountains. Fossils, for example, do not form slowly over millions of years, but rapidly in a quick petrification of tremendous pressure.

Similarly, at the start of the Millennium mountains will be thrown into the sea and valleys raised up. Yet we will still have two eyes and two legs and look like people, not like space creatures or amoebas. As in the time of the flood, conditions will be radically altered, yet some of the basic attributes of man will remain the same.

One Day/One Thousand Years

In discussing the timing of the Second Coming Peter urges us to remember that one day equals a thousand years to God. The one-day, one-thousand-year formula does not apply everywhere, but it does pertain to the coming of the end-times events. A parallel exists between the six days of creation and the six thousand years of human history. The seventh thousand-year period is the

Millennium. The Millennium is parallel to the Sabbath day of rest when comparing history to the week of creation.

We are now nearing the close of six thousand years since the time of Adam. If the model holds true, we are also nearing the start of the millennial Sabbath. The new heavens and new earth after the Millennium are parallel to the Garden of Eden. The Millennium is a one-thousand-year transition between the life we have now and the Garden of Eden-type paradise of the new heavens and new earth. The time from Adam to Noah was a descending transition away from paradise. The time of the Millennium is an upward transition to a paradise restored.

Subduing His Enemies

The people following Adam's time lived almost a thousand years each. As time went on, the lifespan went down and down. As we transition back toward the Millennium and paradise, some people's lifespan will increase.

For as in Adam all die, even so in Christ all shall be made alive. But each one in his own order: Christ the firstfruits, afterward those who are Christ's at His coming. Then comes the end, when He delivers the kingdom to God the Father, when He puts an end to all rule and all authority and power. For He must reign till He has put all enemies under His feet. The last enemy that will be destroyed is death.   1 Corinthians 15:22-26

This is a very significant and clear passage concerning the endtimes. A simple order of events is given: Yeshua is resurrected. Then, after an extended period of time, those who belong to Him are resurrected. Then He begins a period of governmental rule in which all the forces of evil are subdued in a systematic fashion. The last enemy force to be destroyed is "death." At that time comes the final transfer of authority in which Yeshua turns all rule back to God the Father, and Yeshua subordinates Himself to God.

His "coming" here refers to the beginning of the Millennium. *"Those who are Christ's"* refers to those particularly dedicated believers who will rule with Him (cf. Rev. 20:4). The period in which He reigns comes after the resurrection of *"those who are Christ's."* But during that reign the enemies are being subdued. So His coming is at the first resurrection but before the enemies are conquered.

Conquering Death

This first resurrection points to the beginning of the Millennium. Paul clearly states that the time of His coming is at the time of the resurrection of the first group of saints. That is the beginning of the Millennium. Yeshua's coming is also before He rules to put down the enemies of God. That also points to the beginning of the Millennium.

The conquering of death comes at the end of His reign on earth. Yeshua comes; He rules; He conquers evil forces; and finally He conquers death. The period of time between His second coming and the time He delivers the Kingdom to the Father is the Millennium. The Millennium is the period of His ruling, the period of doing away with all evil forces. The Millennium culminates in the abolition of death.

In the Kingdom of God, everything grows in stages like a plant (Mark 4, Matt. 13). During the Millennium the human race will be steadily gaining dominion over all forms of evil—greed, lust, gluttony, fear, sickness, depression, poverty, and so on. (Of course, victory over all these areas is potentially already available to us as believers. We have already been granted every victory through the power of the Spirit and the name of Yeshua—Ephesians 1:3.)

183

Victory Over Death

Although we, as followers of Yeshua, already have access to victory over every area of sin and corruption, the human race as a whole is not experiencing that victory. The Millennium will be a one-thousand-year adjustment to that new life of victory for everyone. People will live prosperously and in health (3 John 2). They will live longer. Since death has not yet been fully conquered (1 Cor. 15:26) or thrown into the lake of fire (Rev. 20:14), people will still die. But the human race as a whole will be gaining advancement even on death.

Any believer in Yeshua could possibly live forever. Yeshua told Peter that it should not matter if He wanted John to stay alive until He returned (John 21:22). Although that is potentially true for an individual, the human race as a whole will have to go through the practical training in faith to openly exercise dominion over death. But that will come at the end of the Millennium. It will take us the whole period of the Millennium to get there, but get there we surely will.

In 1 Corinthians 15, the millennial period is described as the rulership of Yeshua, while the following period of the new heavens and new earth is described as the rulership of God the Father. Yeshua, as the last Adam, brings the human race ultimately back into fellowship and obedience to the Father, even as the first Adam broke that fellowship by disobedience. The first problem was eating the fruit that let the death spirit enter. The last solution will be throwing the death spirit into the fire.

Resurrection Bodies

There are two types of bodies: natural bodies and resurrection bodies.

Someone will say, "How are the dead raised up? And with what body do they come?" Foolish one, what you sow is not made alive unless it dies. And what you sow, you do not sow that body that shall be, but mere grain— perhaps wheat or some other grain.

1 Corinthians 15:35-37

We sometimes have difficulty imagining what it will be like to have a resurrection body. That is only because our minds have been estranged from biblical thinking. We have become fools on what should be a simple matter.

Paul is describing the difference between the natural body and the resurrection body. He uses the example of a seed and the new grain it produces. Our natural body is likened to the old grain; our resurrection body is likened to the life-filled grain that grows up. In other words, our new body will be different, new, filled with life, and not corrupting. On the other hand, it will be similar in size and shape and general configuration to the one we have now.

There are also celestial bodies and terrestrial bodies; but the glory of the celestial is one, and the glory of the terrestrial is another. So also is the resurrection of the dead. The body is sown in corruption, it is raised in in- corruption. It is sown in dishonor, it is raised in glory. It is sown in weakness, it is raised in power.

1 Corinthians 15:40,42-43

Our resurrection bodies will be similar but different. If my body were filled with sickness, and the sickness was suddenly re- moved, my body would go from being a sick body to a healthy one. All preresurrection bodies, even if they are not sick, have been corrupted by death. It is a death-corrupted body. If all the death corruption were to be taken instantly out of your body, you would have an uncorrupted body. The resurrection body is still a human body to a certain extent, but it is one in which all susceptibility to corruption has been removed.

Glorified Bodies

When Moses came off the mountain with God, his body shone with light. He had not been resurrected, but due to so much time in the presence of God, his body began to absorb attributes of a resurrected body. Yeshua appeared to His disciples after the resurrection and ate and walked and talked with them. But He could also disappear and walk through a wall (John 20:26).

When the Bible states that *"flesh and blood cannot inherit the kingdom of God,"* it does not mean that resurrected people do not have a material body of sorts. It is rather contrasting the flesh and blood, mortal, corruptible body with the physical, resurrected, glorified body.

> *Flesh and blood cannot inherit the kingdom of God; nor does corruption inherit incorruption. For this corruptible must put on incorruption, and this mortal must put on immortality.*   1 Corinthians 15:50,53

Our resurrection bodies are physical, but they are not flesh and blood corruptible. The resurrected believers who will reign with Yeshua in the Millennium will have resurrection bodies. Those bodies will have similar capabilities to Yeshua's body after His resurrection. (Not like Lazarus, as Lazarus' resurrection only restored him to health rather than give him a deathless body.)

Post-Resurrection Yeshua

If we want to get a glimpse of what our resurrection bodies will be like, or if we want to get a sense of the people who will rule and reign in the Millennium, we can look to the examples of Yeshua's appearances to His disciples after His resurrection.

Yeshua appeared to them and then disappeared. He was in and out, so to speak. So will be the case with Yeshua and the resurrected believers in the Millennium. The natural people will be living in different locations and traveling by normal means. The resurrected people may not be dwelling permanently at any one location, but will be free to move and appear in different locations as they are led by the Spirit of God.

Yeshua will not be confined to one location in Jerusalem. As He appeared to the disciples at various times, sometimes visible, sometimes not, so will He and His ruling and reigning team of saints move about and visit people during the Millennium.

Natural and Supernatural

Yeshua, in His resurrected body, could walk and talk and eat and be touched physically in all the natural manners. But at His will He could also move supernaturally and override normal physical limitations. So will it be with us in resurrected bodies. We will have available to us all the natural activities that we would like. But we will also be able to move in realms beyond that as we desire.

We will not be formless ghosts or disembodied spirits. We will be real people in real bodies, but we will have at our disposal infinitely greater capacities. You could, theoretically, live in a resurrection body and operate naturally as you do now, if that is what you wanted.

Two Levels

On earth during the Millennium there will be two levels of government. The natural population will have their own society and government that will take care of their own affairs. Cooperating and working with them will be the extraordinary population of resurrected saints, who will act as a team of supernatural special advisors.

Believers will be in all realms of natural government, business, and science. The resurrected saints will be partly like regular citizens and partly like angels acting as helpers as needed.

187

Greater Capacities

Luke 24:36-43 records how Jesus encouraged His disciples to touch Him. He made a point to eat something in their presence. He was doing this to demonstrate to them that the resurrection body is a physical one that can perform all the physical functions. John also records how Jesus encouraged His disciples to touch Him, thus emphasizing the physical aspect of the resurrection and dispelling any strange notions about ghosts and so on.

> *His disciples were again inside....Jesus came, the doors being shut, and stood in their midst, and said, "Peace to you!" Then He said to Thomas, "Reach your finger here, and look at My hands; and reach your hand here, and put it into My side. Do not be unbelieving, but believing."*
>
> John 20:26-27

The resurrection body can be as physical as necessary and as supernatural as necessary. Understanding this twofold dimension can increase your faith.

God did not make a mistake when He designed the human body. What we know of as the human body is in such a degraded state that its capabilities are hardly recognizable. Elijah, for example, was taken up into the air without being harmed (2 Kings 2). Without the taint of sin and death, our bodies could do wonderful things. When Yeshua was on the Mount of Transfiguration, the power of prayer and the Holy Spirit transformed Him until He glowed with radiant light (Matt. 17). That is a good picture of the potential of a sinless, deathless body.

In moments of high glory power, a person with a glorified body may appear as a flash of light to someone looking at him. But actually his form is that of a regular human shape; the brightness of the radiant energy blinded the viewer. For example, if you were to look at someone taking your picture at the exact moment the camera flashed, you could not see the form of the person but only the light flashing out of the bulb. Yeshua, the angels, and any person with a glorified body actually maintains the same basic shape, but their body is capable of radiating brilliant light energy. Wouldn't you like to have your glorified body now?

Mortality Removed

It is not so much the fact that the body has been resurrected that makes the difference, but rather that the corruption elements have been removed and that the new body has been infused with spiritual glory power. Through repentance, prayer, and faith, we can experience a certain degree of that glorification power now.

> *For this corruptible must put on incorruption, and this mortal must put on immortality. So when this corruptible has put on incorruption, and this mortal has put on immortality, then shall be brought to pass the saying that is written: "Death is swallowed up in victory."*
> 1 Corinthians 15:53-54

If this body could be drained of corrupting elements and infused with the electrical glory power of God's Spirit, one would not actually have to die and be resurrected to obtain a resurrection-glorified body.

> *We shall not all sleep* [die]*, but we shall all be changed—in a moment, in the twinkling of an eye...the dead will be raised incorruptible, and we shall be changed.* 1 Corinthians 15:51-52

It even seems that certain Old Testament heroes crossed the lines of mortal limitations of the body: Enoch was translated into Heaven; Moses shone with glory on the mountain; and Elijah was lifted into Heaven.

189

The Promise of Long Life

The key factor is to remove the poison of mortality from this body and infuse it with God's own spiritual energy. A body without mortality would be an immortal body.

As mortality is purged from our midst, people will begin to live longer. Certain passages in the Old Testament promise or indicate increasing longevity.

Moses was one hundred and twenty years old when he died. His eyes were not dim nor his natural vigor diminished. Deuteronomy 34:7

They shall still bear fruit in old age; they shall be fresh and flourishing. Psalm 92:14

Who satisfies your mouth with good things, so that your youth is renewed like the eagle's. Psalm 103:5

The followers of Yeshua who have been particularly dedicated to Him will be given resurrection bodies at His coming and govern this world for a thousand years. The other people living in the Millennium will be at various stages of sanctification: some will operate and live in the fullness of God's glory; some will be immature; and others will actually be against God in their hearts. The rest of the people who have died, whether good or bad, will not be raised until the end of the thousand years, at which time they will receive eternal life or damnation.

Long Life in the Millennium

We are discussing long life and resurrection bodies to help you gain a better image and picture of the millennial period. The following passage clearly connects end-times prophecy with a promise of increasing longevity.

190

*For behold, I create new heavens and a new earth; and
the former shall not be remembered or come to mind.*

Isaiah 65:17

(The new heavens and new earth here is not referring to the
new heavens and new earth at the end of the Millennium as it is
used in Revelation 21, but rather to the general sense of the end-
times including the Millennium, or as it is used in 2 Peter 3.) This
passage contains one of Isaiah's prophetic visions of the beauty of
life in the messianic era.

*No more shall an infant from there live but a few days,
nor an old man who has not fulfilled his days; for the
child shall die one hundred years old, but the sinner
being one hundred years old shall be accursed. For as
the days of a tree, so shall be the days of My people, and
My elect shall long enjoy the work of their hands.*

Isaiah 65:20,22

The reference to the new heavens and new earth shows that
we are dealing with the endtimes. The fact that one hundred years
old would be considered an infant shows that we are dealing with
a later era than our own. The fact that people still die and there are
still sinners present shows that this is before the Great White
Throne Judgment.

Ideal Living Conditions

So we can conclude that this prophetic vision portrays life
after the Second Coming and before the end of the Millennium, that
is to say, in the millennial period itself. As you read the entire passage in Isaiah 65 in context, you will see that this is an era of peace
and joy. The center place of society will be the city of Jerusalem.
People will conduct normal business, work in agriculture and

skilled crafts, give birth to children, raise families, build houses, and so on.

When you combine Isaiah 65 with the ruling and reigning of the resurrected saints in Revelation 20, you have a good picture of the Millennium. The Millennium will feature social justice under the government of the resurrected saints, an absence of war until the last revolt, increased life spans and good health, economic prosperity, and a Jewish-centered calendar and worship format. In other words, the millennial or messianic reign will be a time of peace and prosperity.

Solomon's Kingdom

The closest picture we have of such an ideal kingdom is the society in Israel under King Solomon before he sinned. In his time there was a magnificent temple and worship system in Jerusalem. He enacted international peace agreements among the nations. People enjoyed a fantastic level of financial prosperity. A wise and godly king sat on the throne. Substitute Yeshua for Solomon, and you have a decent rough sketch of millennial conditions in the natural.

So King Solomon was king over all Israel. 1 Kings 4:1

Now Yeshua will be King over Israel, and the greater commonwealth of millennial Israel will extend its sovereignty over all the nations of the world.

And these were his officials: Azariah, the...priest; Elihoreph and Ahijah...scribes; Jehoshaphat...the recorder; Benaiah...over the army...Azariah...over the officers; Zabud...the king's friend; Ahishar, over the household; and Adoniram...over the labor force. And Solomon had twelve governors over all Israel. 1 Kings 4:2-7

When Solomon reigned over such a large territory, he needed a lot of top officials to whom to delegate major areas of government. Likewise, when Yeshua reigns over an international empire, He will employ trusted colleagues to whom He can delegate major areas of authority and responsibility. There will be positions in different levels of authority. Depending on a person's proven record of dependability and service, he will be granted a certain degree of authority.

> *Well done, good and faithful servant; you were faithful over a few things, I will make you ruler over many things. Enter into the joy of your lord.*   Matthew 25:21

> *Well done, good servant; because you were faithful in a very little, have authority over ten cities.*   Luke 19:17

The parable of the minas shows that the reward for faithful dedication to the Lord in this life will be governing authority in the world to come. The more faithful you are here, the more people over whom you will be given leadership authority later. Yeshua will be like a prime minister. Certain believers will be members of His cabinet. Someone will be over the Department of Agriculture. Someone will be in charge of leading the music in the temple. Someone will be mayor of this city or that.

Life in the Kingdom

> *Judah and Israel were as numerous as the sand by the sea in multitude, eating and drinking and rejoicing. So Solomon reigned over all the kingdoms...They brought tribute and served Solomon all the days of his life.*
>
> 1 Kings 4:20-21

The word *Christ* or *Messiah* means "anointed," and it refers to the anointing of a king. In the days of Solomon, each nation or kingdom had its own king, but Solomon was a king even over them. In that way, Solomon was a king of kings.

A king's honor can in some way be measured by the number of people serving him. To Solomon that number was great. To Yeshua as well, the number of people in His Kingdom will be great. There will be an atmosphere of celebration, with people eating and drinking and enjoying themselves. It will be a fun time. People will be happy.

As gold was brought as tribute to Solomon, so will gold be brought to Yeshua as an expression of worship. As the three wise men brought Him gifts at His birth, so will people all over the earth bring gifts to honor Yeshua at His millennial temple. Prosperity during this time will abound.

Since Yeshua will be king over all kingdoms, He will appoint people to positions in authority under Him. Each nation will have its own prime minister or king, if you will, under Yeshua's general reign.

Peace and Prosperity

For he had dominion over all the region...and he had peace on every side all around him. And Judah and Israel dwelt safely, each man under his vine and his fig tree...all the days of Solomon.   1 Kings 4:24-25

No war or lack existed in the Garden of Eden. Whenever the Gospel fully reigns in people's hearts, there comes harmony between people and a restoring of economic provision. The millennial reign will be a time of peace and prosperity. Ultimately, one of the necessary outcomes of the Gospel is peace and prosperity.

The name *Solomon* means "peace" from the root word *shalom*. King Solomon was the king of peace and figure foreshadowing Yeshua Himself. As long as the Prince of Peace is in control, there will be peace. As long as Jehovah Jireh, the Lord our provider, is in control, there will be prosperity.

Each man owned his own fig tree and his own vine. In a certain sense, this means a continuation of the private ownership of property. The millennial reign will not be a communist or socialist state. The vine and fig tree, like the expression "flowing with milk and honey," is a figure of speech meaning "peace and prosperity."

Wisdom

Solomon's wisdom excelled the wisdom of all the men of the East and all the wisdom of Egypt. For he was wiser than all men...and his fame was in all the surrounding nations. He spoke three thousand proverbs, and his songs were one thousand and five. Also he spoke of trees...of animals, of birds, of creeping things, and of fish. And men of all nations, from all the kings of the earth who had heard of his wisdom, came to hear the wisdom of Solomon.   1 Kings 4:30-34

What a beautiful picture of the Millennium this is! Yeshua will teach and speak out of His capital city of Jerusalem. His sermons and wisdom will go forth from there (Isa. 2:3). One of the most enjoyable parts of the millennial Kingdom will be having such access to hear Yeshua.

That wisdom will draw people to Him. What a joy it will be to hear Him give in-depth lessons about different birds and animals and vegetation. Talk about an ecology lesson! It will be like having Thomas Edison change your light bulb, or Henry Ford fix your car!

Hebraic Worship

Perhaps we'll even get an opportunity to sing some songs that Yeshua has written personally. On each of the biblical feast days, representatives from all the nations will come up to Jerusalem to join in the worship.

> *Now three times a year Solomon offered burnt offerings and peace offerings on the altar which he had built for the LORD, and he burned incense with them on the altar that was before the LORD. So he finished the temple.*
>
> 1 Kings 9:25

Scriptures indicate that a magnificent temple will be built during the Millennium (e.g. Ezek. 40ff.). It will be a central place for worship and meeting.

Solomon offered sacrifices three times a year in accordance with the three yearly festivals of *Pesach* (Passover), *Shavuot* (Pentecost or Weeks), and *Sukkot* (Tabernacles). These times of gathering for celebration and dedication will be continued during the Millennium. They will be special times of the manifestation of God's glory.

Yeshua said that true worship is done with the heart in the Spirit, but He also indicated that the ancient Jewish format found in the Bible is the correct one (John 4:22).

Jewish Roots

As biblical standards are established around the world, every area of life will be affected. Interpersonal relationships will improve, as well as public health, the economy, fine arts, and so on. One area that will also be touched is the conforming to a biblical calendar and the ancient Hebraic rhythm of worship and covenant celebrations.

Many Christians have not yet grasped the degree to which certain forms that are Jewish in nature will be part of the millennial Kingdom and a permanent part of God's plan. While we do not have the space or purpose to deal with that topic in depth, we will mention a general overview to be considered:

Temple—Ezekiel 40-48 indicates a divinely ordained temple will be built, including the sacrificial offerings.

Feast of Tabernacles—The nations of the world will all participate in this yearly festival (Zech. 14:16).

Food Laws (Kosher)—Eating swine's flesh or other unclean foods will be considered an abomination (Isa. 66:17).

Sabbath—Each Sabbath everyone in the world will join in for worship. Even the new moon celebrations will be observed (Isa. 66:23).

Passover—Yeshua said that He would partake of the Passover again after His return to earth (Luke 22:18).

Years of Jubilee—Both the seventh-year Sabbath and the fiftieth-year jubilee have never had an opportunity to be observed and fulfilled (Lev. 25).

Pentecost (Feast of Weeks)—This holy day has end-times significance and has already been incorporated in many Christian circles as a special time for the outpouring of God's Spirit (Acts 2).

Torah (Law of Moses)—The teachings of the Law of Moses are not to be done away with (Matt. 5:17) and will be part of the teaching ministry of the endtimes (Isa. 2:3).

Jerusalem—Whether during the Millennium or the new heavens and new earth, Jerusalem will remain the center of life on earth (Rev. 21).

Jewish Roots—Christianity and Judaism will be seen as a single tree whose roots and branches have been grafted together (Rom. 11).

Israel and the Nations

During the reign of Solomon, a certain international order or harmony of the nations prevailed, with Israel as the head among her sister nations. So will it be in the Millennium. God has assigned each nation or people group on the face of the earth a certain place to live (Acts 17:26). These people groups and homeland assignments are broken down into seventy divisions (Deut. 32:8).

Note: These seventy nation groups are matched symbolically by the seventy sons of Jacob, the seventy bulls sacrificed at the Feast of Tabernacles, and the seventy disciples that were sent out by Yeshua. Twelve refers to Israel; seventy refers to the nations.

Part of the total restoration of the world order in the endtimes will be to have the Jews living in Israel and the other people groups living in their assigned territories. To some degree, America and Israel may be exceptions to that rule.

America, while I have no Scriptures to prove it, seems to be a special haven for people of all different nationalities. I believe that is a sovereign work of God and will continue in some way. In addition, using Ruth and Rahab as examples, the Scriptures show that any person from any nationality group may choose to identify himself or herself more closely in kinship with the Jewish people and be welcomed to take his or her place as an equal member in the tribes of Israel.

The Messianic Kingdom

Isaiah 2 contains a beautiful poetic description, a prophetic vision, of the Messiah's Kingdom. Peace among the nations, justice, and the reestablishment of Israel comprised the hope that motivated and inspired the prophets over the centuries.

In the mind of the prophets, peace and justice in the world were intricately connected with the restoration of Israel as a nation.

Now it shall come to pass in the latter days that the mountain of the LORD'S house shall be established on

the top of the mountains, and shall be exalted above the
hills; and all nations shall flow to it.   Isaiah 2:2

This is symbolic language referring to Israel's regaining of her place of leadership within the international community of nations.

Come, and let us go up to the mountain of the LORD, to
the house of the God of Jacob....For out of Zion shall go
forth the law, and the word of the LORD from Jerusalem.
    Isaiah 2:3

Jerusalem and the temple there will be reestablished as a worldwide spiritual center. People will gather there for worship and teaching. Revelational instruction and authoritative doctrine will go out from Jerusalem to all nations.

He shall judge between the nations, and rebuke many
people; they shall beat their swords into plowshares,
and their spears into pruning hooks; nation shall not
lift up sword against nation, neither shall they learn
war anymore.   Isaiah 2:4

The result of Israel's being reestablished as the head of the nations is that justice and judgment can then be exercised to those nations. Israel in right order means justice in right order. Justice in right order brings peace. Therefore the reestablishment of Israel is a necessary ingredient to restoring peace to the world.

The Messiah restores Israel. Israel brings justice and order to the nations. Justice and order results in world peace. These different themes are woven into one fabric in the vision of the messianic Kingdom.

The Prophets' Vision

Isaiah 11 is also a prophetic portrait of the millennial Kingdom.

There shall come forth a Rod from the stem of Jesse,
and a Branch shall grow out of his roots.   Isaiah 11:1

This branch is a poetic description of Yeshua the Messiah arising out of the lineage of King David. The passage continues by speaking of the Messiah's anointing for wisdom and good counsel.

With righteousness He shall judge the poor, and decide
with equity for the meek of the earth; he shall strike the
earth with the rod of His mouth, and with the breath of
His lips He shall slay the wicked.   Isaiah 11:4

Again we see the theme of justice restored. The teachings, judgments, and pronouncements of the Messiah will be so authoritative that justice will prevail. The Messiah brings justice, and that justice results in peace.

The wolf also shall dwell with the lamb, the leopard
shall lie down with the young goat, the calf and the
young lion and the fatling together; and a little child
shall lead them. The nursing child shall play by the
cobra's hole, and the weaned child shall put his hand in
the viper's den. They shall not hurt nor destroy in all My
holy mountain, for the earth shall be full of the knowl-
edge of the LORD as the waters cover the sea.

Isaiah 11:6,8-9

How beautiful! This is the hope of Israel, the dream of the prophets. The Messiah, His teachings, justice, and peace are all wrapped up together. Once again, this vision for world peace is based upon the regathering and reestablishment of Israel.

The Lord shall set His hand again the second time to re-
cover the remnant of His people who are left....He will
set up a banner for the nations, and will assemble the

outcasts of Israel, and gather together the dispersed of
Judah from the four corners of the earth.

Isaiah 11:11-12

This prophecy concerns Yeshua the Messiah and His work in the endtimes to establish His Kingdom on the earth. A major section of this end-times prophecy about Yeshua deals with His regathering of the Jewish people to Israel. It is Yeshua Himself who is supervising the return of the Jewish people to Israel in our day. It is a fulfillment of prophecy. An essential and intrinsic part of believing in Yeshua in these endtimes is to believe in the restoration of Israel as a sovereign work of God.

Visualizing World Peace

We all want peace. But peace demands justice. And justice demands the restitution of the Jewish nation. Peace comes when justice prevails. Justice involves the punishment of the wicked and the restoration of the innocent. There is no peace until wrongs are righted.

Yeshua is the Son of God, but He is also the Son of David. He is the Savior of the world, but He is also the King of the Jews.

The Millennium is a jigsaw puzzle that the Lord is putting together. The pieces of the picture include Yeshua, Israel, peace, justice, and wisdom. That is the world peace we are visualizing. That is the vision of the prophets.

CHAPTER 7

REBUILDING THE TEMPLE

by Keith Intrater

Rabbinic Authority

Many are asking whether a third temple will be built in Jerusalem in the near future. If a temple were to be built, it would be engineered primarily by the orthodox rabbinic community. Certainly many Christians and Jewish believers in Yeshua would be involved in the construction, but the legal authority for the project would remain with the rabbis.

To a certain extent, this legal authority for building the temple and supervising the practical administering of the Mosaic ordinances is an authority granted by God.

> Then Jesus spoke to the multitudes and to His disciples, saying: "The scribes and the Pharisees sit in Moses' seat. Therefore whatever they tell you to observe, that observe and do, but do not do according to their works..." Matthew 23:1-3

The rabbinic community may be seen as the extension of the scribes and Pharisees. Notice that Yeshua affirmed their authority dealing with the Mosaic Law. He made this statement both to the general Israeli populace and to His own followers.

If we are to answer the question as to how, when, and if a third temple will be built, we must come to an understanding of the orthodox rabbinic view of the endtimes and the Messiah.

God's Temple

Remember that the tabernacle and temple sacrificial system was originally given directly to Moses and David by God Himself. The authority to operate the code of laws was given to the priestly tribe in Israel. Other people were anointed as prophets and kings and artisans, but the authority for the sacrifices was given to the tribe of Levi. Yeshua accepted the continuance of that delegated authority of the scribes and Pharisees even though they were grossly misusing their position.

How can God use people who are not believers in Yeshua to build a temple and even fulfill prophecy? Let us recall that the majority of the scribes and Pharisees in Yeshua's time were not followers of Him either. Yeshua made that statement to His disciples as well. In addition, God used a Gentile king named Cyrus to foster the building of the second temple.

New Covenant Priesthood

Furthermore, as we understand it, there are two priestly systems of worship. The first is the spiritual one in Heaven, in which any believer in Yeshua, whether Jew or Greek, has equal access. The other is the physical model and representation of the heavenly temple, whose symbols and sacrifices are governed under God by the Jewish people here on earth. When a person becomes a believer in Yeshua, he participates in the heavenly priesthood, and the earthly sacrifices are relegated to secondary importance, only a shadow and symbol of the real thing. To that extent, the levitical priesthood is virtually passed away, other than its value as a visual aid to worship, a symbolic action of faith, and a sign of God's historic faithfulness to His covenant with the Jewish people.

In that He says, "A new covenant," He has made the first obsolete. Now what is becoming obsolete and growing old is ready to vanish away. Hebrews 8:13

For a believer in Yeshua, the old covenant symbols are becoming obsolete as he experiences the reality of supernatural heavenly worship. They are ready to vanish but have not yet vanished. While their importance is now secondary and temporary, there is an era of significance remaining.

Dual Meaning

For the rest of the Jewish community and even the international non-Christian community, the historic witness of the Mosaic system and symbolic atonement maintains a primary importance demonstrating God's faithfulness, sovereignty, and holiness.

> *It was symbolic for the present time in which both gifts and sacrifices are offered which cannot make him who performed the service perfect in regard to the conscience— concerned only with foods and drinks, various washings, and fleshly ordinances imposed until the time of reformation.* Hebrews 9:9-10

Again we see that the temple system cannot provide a spiritually perfect cleansing for the conscience, but it does provide a service of symbolic demonstration. At the present time, we are in a transition period. Ultimately there will be no need for a temple at all, because the heavenly worship area will actually descend to earth, and the heavenly and earthly worship will be merged.

> *Behold, the tabernacle of God is with men, and He will dwell with them...But I saw no temple in it, for the Lord God Almighty and the Lamb are its temple.* Revelation 21:3,22

Before the time of Yeshua, the temple sacrifices were the primary vehicle on earth for receiving atonement and forgiveness. In the future new heavens and new earth, there will be no temple at all. Until then, in our present age, the temple has a fading, less significant role for believers in Yeshua, and a continuing historic and symbolic importance for the Jewish people and the rest of the world.

> *For the law, having a shadow of the good things to come, and not the very image of the things, can never with these same sacrifices, which they offer continually year by year, make those who approach perfect.*
>
> Hebrews 10:1

We must maintain a balance in our appreciation of the temple. It is not the means of itself by which a person can be reborn spiritually and transformed in the inner man. It is a mere symbolic vehicle that is being done away with. On the other hand, it is not a detestable abomination that must be cast out of the presence of God. It was designed by God, it has symbolic meaning, and it has prophecies concerning it that are yet unfulfilled.

The Challenge of Hebrews

Since the writer of Hebrews states that the sacrifices are presently being offered every year, it is clear that the letter was written before the destruction of the temple in 70 A.D. Not only does this fact give us evidence for the early and valid composition of the letter, but it also gives us a contextual idea of the issue the writer was addressing.

The letter was written to Jewish believers in Yeshua who were still quite involved in the temple. The impact and aura of the temple was so powerful on an emotional level that the Jewish believers were in danger of losing their perspective on how fully Yeshua effected redemption for them. The majesty of the temple was so attractive that they were in danger of becoming attached to the rituals and forgetting that the temple sacrifices were merely symbolic.

The writer challenges them to put their faith in what Yeshua accomplished for them in the heavenlies. He warns the first-century believers not to attach more significance to the sacrifices than their intended symbolic meaning. It is clear therefore that the believers in Yeshua in the first century were attending the temple and participating *en masse* in the temple celebrations. They are not told to avoid the temple, but only not to become attached to it emotionally, and not to give it more importance than is due.

Balanced Perspective

To understand the prophecies of the endtimes concerning the temple, we must have the same balanced perspective. To see more importance in the temple than is due can cause a person to weaken his faith and even be deceived to the point of denying the completed work of redemption in Yeshua's death and resurrection. On the other hand, if we reject everything connected with the temple as an abomination, we will not be able to understand the prophecies concerning the temple and its role in the endtimes.

As with anything physical, whether it be the environment, our bodies, politics, or money, we cannot let it take priority over spiritual issues. On the other hand, if we do not approach natural things with an application of biblical principles, we will lose an understanding of God's will concerning them.

No Psychological Attachment

So it is with the temple. So it was with the disciples of Yeshua in the time of the second temple.

> Then as He went out of the temple, one of His disciples said to Him, "Teacher, see what manner of stones and what buildings are here!"   Mark 13:1

Jesus had been with His disciples teaching in the temple. One disciple commented to Him how impressive were the blocks of stone and massive architecture of the temple. He was appealing to an emotionalism to get Yeshua impressed as well. (Anyone who has been to the temple excavations in Jerusalem can sense the emotional pull and impressiveness of the temple works.)

And Jesus answered and said to him, "Do you see these great buildings? Not one stone shall be left upon another, that shall not be thrown down."   Mark 13:2

Yeshua sensed the disciples' psychological attachment to the physical buildings. Their feelings were representative of the whole nation. The people of Israel had begun to put the impressiveness of outward religion in front of their heart relationship with God. This was disastrous for the nation and particularly dangerous for Yeshua's own disciples.

Lust Destroys

In a certain sense, the attachment to outward religion was at the core of Israel's downfall, both spiritually and nationally. It is a biblical principle that whatever part of life one grasps onto and becomes soulishly attached to—he loses. Greed ultimately leads to corruption. Lust ultimately leads to marital breakdown.

Yeshua's prophecy that the temple would be destroyed was not just a mystical statement about God's sovereignty; it was a reflection of spiritual cause and effect. Yeshua knew the spiritual principle that applied: what a man holds onto he will lose. What the nation of Israel (including the disciples of Yeshua) were holding onto would soon be destroyed.

This prophecy was predominantly fulfilled in 70 A.D. when the Roman army destroyed Jerusalem. The root cause of the destruction, however, was not the Roman army but the religious pride, hypocrisy, and psychological attachment to outward form on the part of the Jewish people. (Of course, the same could be said of almost every revival of Christendom that later became fossilized into stale denominationalism.)

The Jewish people caused the destruction of the temple by their own pride and lust for it. Whenever we lust for something or become psychologically attached to it, we release a force of corruption that will soon destroy it (2 Pet. 1:4, Prov. 11:24, John 12:25).

Witness in the Temple

Jesus did indeed warn His disciples not to be impressed by the temple building and its worship. However, after His resurrection, the disciples were involved in the temple events.

> *Now Peter and John went up together to the temple at the hour of prayer, the ninth hour.*　　　Acts 3:1

The Jewish people used the daily afternoon sacrifice time as a special period for prayer. The disciples were going up to the temple at that time to pray. This time they were not fixated on the temple structures but were, rather, sensitive to the words of Yeshua.

Through that spiritual perceptiveness they took notice of a man in need of healing. The man was healed miraculously by the name of Jesus through the hands of Peter. He then went leaping and praising God right through the temple itself.

> *So he, leaping up, stood and walked and entered the temple with them—walking, leaping, and praising God.*
> 　　　Acts 3:8

You can imagine the effect this wondrous miracle had on the people in the temple. It was a remarkable testimony both to the people and to the priests.

Interacting With the Temple

This was similar to Yeshua's technique in that often when He healed someone, He would send them to the temple to offer the appropriate Mosaic sacrifice as a testimony to the priests (Matt. 8:4).

This is also how it will be in the endtimes. The Jewish believers in Jesus will cooperate and participate in the general format of temple events. But they will be more interested in healings and miraculous testimonies than in the temple practices per se. The evidence of miracles and preaching in the temple area will be a witness and testimony to the orthodox Jewish community.

The interaction between the disciples and the temple priesthood in the first century serves as a model, foreshadowing similar interactions in the endtimes.

Preaching and Persecution

The early disciples participated in the temple activities. They were not overly impressed by the grandeur of the priesthood. They had their eye on preaching, prayer, and miracles. In addition, they also met with tremendous persecution and opposition on behalf of the Jewish religious authorities. This pattern of persecution must not be forgotten.

> *Now as they* [the disciples] *spoke to the people, the priests, the captain of the temple, and the Sadducees came upon them. And they laid hands on them, and put them in custody until the next day....However, many of those who heard the word believed; and the number of the men came to be about five thousand.*   Acts 4:1,3-4

So it will be in the endtimes. Many will be saved. Miracles will take place. Confrontation and preaching will happen right in the temple area. The religious authorities will be angry and reach out to stop the believers.

On the next day Peter and John were able to share their testimony before all the gathered leaders of the Jewish community

(vv. 5-6). The leaders chastised Peter and John and told them not to preach anymore.

> *So they called them and commanded them not to speak at all nor teach in the name of Jesus. But Peter and John answered and said to them, "Whether it is right in the sight of God to listen to you more than to God, you judge. For we cannot but speak the things which we have seen and heard."*   Acts 4:18-20

Two levels of authority are represented here. The religious leaders have the delegated authority to operate the temple system. Peter and John try to cooperate as much as possible with that authority. On the other hand, they are under the direct authority of God.

When the disciples are under the legitimate operation of the temple, they submit and cooperate. However, when the religious authorities overstep their bounds and tell the disciples not to preach, the disciples disobey them and reject their orders to their face.

This is a similar dynamic to what any Christian would face in dealing with the police. When the government acts legitimately, to set traffic laws, for instance, every believer should obey. If the government commands a believer to renounce his faith, however, he should defy the government openly. As Christians deal with secular authority today, so will the end-times believers react to the temple authorities in the years to come.

Confrontation and Miracles

The disciples are repeatedly punished and imprisoned, yet they continue to preach, returning by divine mandate.

> [They] *laid their hands on the apostles and put them in the common prison. But at night an angel of the Lord*

opened the prison doors and brought them out, and
said, "Go, stand in the temple and speak to the people
all the words of this life."   Acts 5:18

And so the cycle continues: preaching, miracles, and imprisonment. The end-times believers will be able to participate in temple functions and at the same time provide a supernatural witness to the people of Jerusalem.

Although the opposition was and will be strong, so are the results. Even some of the priests and Levites performing the sacrifices will come to know Yeshua and offer the sacrifices with a reborn heart.

The number of the disciples multiplied greatly in
Jerusalem, and a great many of the priests were obedi-
ent to the faith.   Acts 6:7

What a wonderful picture of revival this is! Imagine Jewish believers in Yeshua leading the Jewish temple worship in Jerusalem.

The apostle Paul showed a similar deference in his interaction with temple authority. At one point he preaches in the temple itself to the point of causing a riot (Acts 22:22). At another time he debates with the high priest, yet politely submits to his authority (Acts 23:5). At another point he goes up to the temple to fulfill one of the strictest vows of the Old Covenant and offer sacrifices (Acts 21:26).

The actions of the Jewish believers in Yeshua in the Book of Acts, in relation to the temple, provide an example of how it may happen in the endtimes.

When Daniel was in Babylon during the first exile, he timed his prayer schedule to match the sacrificial system, even though the temple had been destroyed (Dan. 6:10; 9:21). Among Christians everywhere, the feasts of Israel, such as Tabernacles,

Passover, and Pentecost, have always been a focal point for times of special prayer and the moving of the Holy Spirit.

Failure of Secular Zionism

Since the operation of the temple system has been delegated to the rabbis and Levites, we need to understand how orthodox Judaism sees the endtimes if we are to understand the prophecies concerning the temple.

There have been two major philosophies in bringing the Jews back to Israel in modern times (other than the Christian or prophetic view). Among the majority of the Jewish people, these may be seen as secular Zionism and religious Zionism.

Secular Zionism based its philosophy on the nationalism, enlightenment, and socialism that arose out of Europe in the late nineteenth century. It was primarily a humanistic argument that said: Since all other people groups have a nation and are equal among the international fraternity of nations, so should the Jews. Zionism was a parallel to the national identity movements among other peoples.

So secular Zionism is a movement based on human rights. It found exponential sympathy for itself in the wake of the Holocaust. In recent years, with the subtle misrepresentation of the Palestinian issue, sympathy for the Jews based on equal rights has been deteriorating. Actually the facts concerning the Arab-Israeli conflict still throw human rights in favor of Israel, but the media propaganda has eroded popular opinion away from that moral argument both in Israel and abroad. And with each passing year away from World War II, the general public is forgetting the moral lessons learned from the Holocaust.

In other words, the humanistic philosophical base on which secular Zionism was founded will ultimately turn against Israel. It is only a matter of time.

Religious Zionism

The religious argument refers back to an incontestable right to the land based on God's covenant with Abraham. The orthodox religious establishment does believe in a divine mandate to own the land. Therefore its philosophical base will not be undermined by political considerations. It must be remembered, however, that the orthodox rabbinic establishment is also strongly opposed to any belief in Yeshua. The Bible says that while they are loved by God because of their kinship with Abraham, they themselves are outright enemies of the Gospel (Rom. 11:28).

Until now the religious wing in Israel has been a minority. In the long run their numbers are likely to increase. Because of their religious framework, they are having more children. The religious convictions of the orthodox are a stronger motivation to withstand the hardships and discomforts of living in Israel. A secular Jew from America is not as likely to immigrate to Israel in the present circumstances as a religious one.

New Mainstream

One exception to this categorizing is the influx of Russian Jews. The Russian Jews are not religious, but they are coming in great numbers to escape persecution in Russia. Both Isaiah (43:6) and Jeremiah (23:8) prophesied this Russian immigration.

In summary, secular Zionism is facing a crisis because its appeals for support based on national equality are being undermined by international support for demands of the Palestinians for their own national equality. The orthodox are likely to increase proportionately in numbers because of their religious convictions to have children and their belief in a divine mandate for the land.

Between the two extremes is emerging an Israeli conservative mainstream who believe generally in God's providence over Israel and in her case for social justice, but who are not caught up either in liberal humanism or rabbinic legalism. These mainstream, moderate Israelis represent a hope for the future of the nation.

Failure of Western Culture

Orthodox Judaism, like its counterparts in Islam, sees a deep-seated failure of Western culture. They rightly see the breakdown of sexual and family values, the rejection of religion and authority, the decadent lifestyles, and the atheistic philosophies. Both Islam and rabbinic Judaism feel confirmed in their dogmatism as they compare themselves to the decadence and humanism in Western (and in their minds, Christian) culture.

Divine Jurisdiction

Rabbinic Judaism, much like Catholicism, sees divine authority as invested in the long-standing structure of the clergy. Rabbinic Judaism would not approve of a person reading his Bible individually and asking for divine guidance on application of the Scriptures. Instead, it has a compilation of rabbinic interpretations and judicial decisions, called the Talmud, that is received with equal authority to the Scriptures. Rabbinic jurisdiction influences the Jews' understanding of the Messiah. Since the rabbinic council is invested with divine jurisdiction in religious matters, the rabbis could not possibly make a mistake in recognizing and confirming who the Messiah is. The rabbis in the Sanhedrin council determined that Yeshua was not the Messiah, and since they have the legal right to determine that choice, by definition Yeshua cannot be the Messiah. Or so the logic goes.

The same jurisdiction applies in reverse. How, it may be asked, will the Jewish people ever receive the Messiah? At the right time and by appropriate standards, the rabbinic council will recognize and confirm who the messiah is, and that will be the correct choice.

Orthodox Messiah

It must be remembered that the rabbinic view is not seeking to impose divine, "Son of God" standards on their messiah. To them, the messiah will be a man of prophetic anointing like Elijah, a military victor like David, and a wise politician like Solomon. He will be a religious king, a man of great stature. As the Catholics see the pope, and the Muslims see their Ayatollah, so will the orthodox Jews give veneration to their coming messiah.

In other words, a Jewish man with a charismatic personality, who is a leader within rabbinic orthodoxy, and who leads Israel in political unity and military victory would be a good candidate. The rabbinic council would simply have to identify such a hero and give him their stamp of approval, and there you have it: a messiah. That is not at all outside the scope of possibility in the near future.

Plan of Salvation

The orthodox rabbinic establishment plans to take control of the nation of Israel in a very practical way. They have political parties and seek to parlay their influence into increasing power. They seek now particularly to control such elements as immigration, marriage authority, transportation, and education. They want to see the entire country submitted under rabbinic law and rabbinic authority, which they regard as the appropriate extension of God's authority.

A simplified view of their plan to save the world is the following: The world is in trouble because it is disobeying God's Law (the Torah). If Israel would obey the Torah, she would become a shining light and a leader to the rest of the nations. Then the rest of the nations would be drawn to obey God's laws. The world would be restored to an ideal state.

Since the rabbis are invested with the authority to administrate the Torah, what they are seeking is for all Israel to submit to rabbinic law. That, in turn, would be the propelling force to bring the world into restoration. So when it is all boiled down, they believe the world will be saved by getting the Jewish people in Israel to obey the laws of God as they are interpreted by the rabbis.

If Israel would submit to rabbinic authority, the world would be saved. That is why they are so zealous to get all the Jews in Israel to obey rabbinic tradition. They are out to save the world; they have their plan to do so and are energetically pursuing that plan.

The Teshuvah Movement

The rabbis are out to convert thousands of Israelis to orthodox Judaism. They are aggressively pursuing that goal. This zeal for conversion is called the *Ba'al Teshuvah* movement. The term means "master of repentance." Repentance in orthodox Judaism is seen as a return to the rabbinic traditions, such as the kosher food laws, the phylacteries (*tephilin*), and keeping the Sabbath. A person who has repented, therefore, is a person who has returned to practicing the traditional Jewish lifestyle.

When enough people have repented—that is, when enough people have returned to an orthodox lifestyle—the messiah will come. In a messianic prophecy, Isaiah said that the redeemer would come to those who turn from transgression in Jacob (Isa. 59:20). Paul quotes this, saying that the deliverer will come and turn away ungodliness from Jacob (Rom. 11:26).

Christians would see this to mean that the catastrophic events leading up to the second coming of Yeshua will cause many Jewish people to accept Him as their Savior. To a certain extent Yeshua will not return until the Jews turn to Him.

Rabbinic Judaism sees that the messiah will not come until enough Jews have repented—or returned to orthodox practices.

They zealously seek to convert Jews to orthodox practice (*halachah*) so that the messiah can come. Christians, of course, are hoping to see Jews come to know Yeshua before He returns.

Obeying the Law

Don't the rabbis believe in a loving personal relationship with God? Yes, they would answer, but love for God is primarily demonstrated through obeying the laws. The laws are in the hands of rabbinic tradition. Therefore, to love God is to obey the traditions.

So the rabbis believe that the messiah will not come unless they can get a large number of Jews to practice the traditions. The rabbinic scheme for the endtimes is the following:

1. Convert the Jews in Israel to orthodox Judaism
2. Take over the Israeli government
3. Impose rabbinic law in Israel
4. Convert millions of Gentiles to Judaism
5. Declare a messiah
6. The messiah will rebuild the temple
7. All nations will submit to rabbinic law

From these steps they believe the world will emerge into peace and prosperity under God.

Gentile Converts

How will millions of Gentiles become orthodox Jews? The masses of Gentiles will not have to maintain all the rituals of orthodoxy, but only adhere to a few laws that express the fundamental moral principles. Those essential morals are called the Noachide laws (Gen. 9). Millions of Gentiles will be converted, not as orthodox Jews, but as righteous proselytes with a minimum number of prerequisites.

The acceptance of minimum requirements for righteous proselytes is somewhat similar to the decision made by James and the apostolic council (Acts 15) in the New Testament.

Building the Temple

Are the orthodox Jews planning to build a temple? Absolutely. There are groups even now in Israel working on plans for a temple. But the temple can only be built under divine inspiration, the rabbis acknowledge. The only person who will have the prophetic anointing to supervise the building of the temple is the messiah, say the rabbis. Therefore the temple cannot be built until the messiah comes.

The Christian mind might jump at this point and think, "The temple cannot be built until after Yeshua returns." But the orthodox Jews are not looking for Yeshua; they are looking for their own portrait of a messiah.

Should there be an attack on Israel in the near future, and Israel be victorious, and should a war hero emerge who is a devoutly orthodox man, the rabbinic council could recognize him as the messiah and affirm his prophetic insight to oversee the construction of the temple. Then the temple could be built.

Priests from the tribe of Levi would be needed to conduct the sacrifices. But how could anyone be sure their genealogies were valid? Again, the rabbinic court would conduct a reasonable certification program and verify the priests and Levites with divine unction.

In the case of large numbers of sacrifices needed to be performed, assistants could be appointed under the supervision of certified priests (2 Chron. 29:34).

For the thousands of potential international visitors, the many sacrifices would be done outside in the open courtyard. The temple building itself does not have to be very large. When the people returned to Israel from Babylon with Zerubbabel, they simply set up an altar on the ground and offered sacrifices (Ezra 3:2). The temple building itself was not constructed until later.

A Scenario

In summary, humanistic Zionism is eroding. The orthodox establishment will gain in power and numbers. A new mainstream of Israelis will emerge who see God's hand upon the nation, but who are not embroiled in orthodox dogmatism.

An international war will break out against Israel involving a coalition of European and Arab states. A miraculous victory for Israel will take place. A strong orthodox power base will recognize a leader from that war as the messiah. He will serve as a combination king, prime minister, and chief rabbi.

Unity and peace will be brought to the country. In the aftermath of the war, a stunned peace settles over the Middle East and Europe. The temple mount area is cleared. Sacrifices begin. Construction of a new temple begins.

Money pours in from all over the world for the temple. Tourists and religious pilgrims from around the world come to Israel. Israel emerges as an international leader, both economically and politically. God's grace and favor are unmistakably upon the nation.

The chief rabbi-prime minister becomes a popular world figure. Thousands of nominal Christians choose to become proselytes to Judaism under the lenient Noachide ordinances. True Christians search their Scriptures to understand the Jewish roots of their faith and the implications of end-times prophecies.

Revivals and persecutions happen around the world. Jewish believers in Yeshua in Israel preach openly in the streets, accompanied by miracles. The orthodox establishment brands them as a cult and tries to imprison them, but popular resistance won't allow it. Miracles and persecutions happen at the same time.

Rabbinic Judaism has the opportunity to run the country as it desires. Positive results, such as the solidification of family life, reduction of crime, and economic improvement occur. The rabbinic council begin to spread their dream of an orthodox Jewish redemption and messianic era.

Problems in the Scenario

The messiah-prime minister is a sincere man and wins the hearts of many. Many Christians take him to be the antichrist but are mistaken in this evaluation. All goes well for a few years, but then certain things go sour.

Eastern-New Age mysticism continues to spread and increase. Islamic fundamentalism continues to grow. The old tensions between Arab and Jew in Israel remain bitter. A backlash of anti-Semitism in Europe starts swelling. The orthodox utopia reveals some cracks in its foundations. Power struggles and hypocrisy manifest in the orthodox political and religious establishment. The fundamental problems on the international scene have not been dealt with. Many young Israelis become disillusioned with the orthodoxy but search for God's reality in their lives.

Revival and miracles spread even more around the world, as well as fiercer opposition to them. A satanic economic and political power structure emerges out of Europe. World tensions grow to a high mark. The stage is set for a final series of horribly distressful world events. The messiah-prime minister begins to be involved in New Age practices and mixes this Eastern mysticism and occult with his Judaism.

The combined political and military forces of Europe, Russia, Africa, and the Arab world begin to move against Israel. Widespread revival and intensive persecution continue around the world. An international invasion is launched against Israel. Pressure mounts. Many Israelis cry out to know Yeshua. Miracles and angelic appearances proliferate. The war closes in. Nuclear weapons are unleashed.

Such is a possible scenario of how events could progress in Israel in line with end-times prophecies and the religious agenda of orthodox Jews. It is meant to prod your thinking in a biblical direction. Virtually all theological schemes will be found defective as we approach these tumultuous times.

Vision of the Temple

It is difficult for many Christians to conceive that the building of a temple in the endtimes is actually a part of God's plan. Ezekiel had a vision of an end-times temple and of a man measuring its dimensions.

> *Behold, there was a man whose appearance was like the appearance of bronze. He had a line of flax and a measuring rod in his hand....Now there was a wall all around the outside of the temple. In the man's hand was a measuring rod six cubits long, each being a cubit and a handbreadth; and he measured the width of the wall structure, one rod; and the height, one rod.*
>
> Ezekiel 40:3,5

Ezekiel was to take careful note of this vision and report it to the people of Israel in captivity. The vision was designed to spark them to return to God.

John, in Revelation, received a quite similar vision, also seeing a man with a measuring rod.

> *Then I was given a reed like a measuring rod. And the angel stood, saying, "Rise and measure the temple of God, the altar, and those who worship there. But leave out the court which is outside the temple, and do not measure it, for it has been given to the Gentiles. And they will tread the holy city underfoot for forty-two months."*
>
> Revelation 11:1

222

Here we have John himself measuring the temple. This is a temple that did not exist during the first century. It is standing while there is yet much tribulation to occur before the start of the Millennium. So a prophetically ordained temple will be built long after the time of Yeshua, but before the millennial age, and right in the midst of the turmoil of the Book of Revelation.

The Power of Orthodoxy

The orthodox Jewish establishment is a powerful force. It will be used of God to build the temple. Yet its adherents stand in direct opposition to the Gospel. The apostle Paul came from a strict Pharisee background, persecuted believers, and then gave his life to the Lord.

Yeshua's most difficult struggles in the Bible were not with sinners, prostitutes, or the demon-possessed. His most vehement confrontations were with the stubborn and hypocritical religious leaders. Yeshua's greatest attacks were those that came from the Pharisees. The force of tradition on the human mind is powerful and must always be resisted.

Hitler attacked the orthodox communities of Eastern Europe. But today Hitler is gone and Israel is alive. Russian communism rose and fell in mere moments of time when compared to the continuance of Jewish tradition. Other religions have come and gone.

Rabbinic Judaism may be the single oldest cultural or historical entity in the history of man.

> *Concerning the gospel they are enemies for your sake, but concerning the election they are beloved for the sake of the fathers.*   Romans 11:28

Purposes of the End-Times Temple

The end-times temple will serve as a sign of God's power to scatter and regather the nation of Israel. The destruction of the temple in 70 A.D. and its rebuilding two thousand years later is a witness to God's sovereignty and omnipotence.

The temple will also serve as a point of contention for the ungodly nations and false religions. This classic symbol of the ancient biblical faith will be a stumbling block of offense to everyone of humanistic orientation.

Thirdly, the temple will be an opportunity for the orthodox to have their day in court, as it were. After all these years of exile, the temple will be a testing ground for them to demonstrate the positive aspects of the Mosaic Law and to what extent religious hypocrisy has been cleansed from their midst.

Finally, the temple is a symbol to believers in Yeshua everywhere of God's plan to graft the branches back into the tree (Rom. 11) and to bring all things back under one head (Eph. 1:10). The last will be first, and now what was first will come full circle to being the last.

The temple will ultimately be a place of unity, purity, beauty, and worship. Yeshua called it *"My Father's house"* (John 2:16-17). It is God's footstool (Ps. 99:5). It is the sign of God's covenant with David, as circumcision is Abraham's sign and the rainbow Noah's. First the temple will be built physically. Then it will be purified to fulfill all its purposes spiritually (1 Cor. 15:46). That is God's pattern, first the natural, then the spiritual.

The Hope of Two Thousand Years

The Jewish prayer service is repeated by all observant men twice daily, morning and evening. Generally speaking, the men gather together in the synagogue both before work and after. The central prayer of that twice-a-day prayer service is a list of eighteen prayers called the *shmonah-esreh* or "the Eighteen."

To follow the orthodox way of thinking, it is significant to notice the order of some of these prayers.

224

10) The tenth prayer requests the regathering of the Jewish people from the four corners of the earth back to the land of Israel.

14) The fourteenth prayer asks for the return of the city of Jerusalem to the Jewish people.

15) The fifteenth prayer asks for the coming of the Messiah.

17) The seventeenth prayer asks for the rebuilding of the temple with the restoration of the temple worship system.

Isn't that significant? Notice the order: the regathering to Israel—the recapture of Jerusalem—the coming of the Messiah—the rebuilding of the temple. There you have it: Israel, then Jerusalem, then Messiah, then the temple.

This prayer has been repeated by orthodox Jewish men all over the world in unison and agreement twice daily for nearly two thousand years. Imagine the effect of that. Their hopes of two thousand years are in the process of coming to pass. Let us pray for their eyes to be opened to the truth of Messiah Yeshua in these Last Days.

CHAPTER 8

THE BOOK OF REVELATION
AND THE EXODUS

by Daniel Juster

A Response to Chapter 7

Do I believe, concerning the Tribulation, that the establishment of a Tribulation temple, an orthodox victory in Ezekiel 37
and 38, and an orthodox period in the early part of the Tribulation
are biblically provable? Now I am coming, as a teacher, between
that which is solidly clear in the Word and that which is spiritual
and reasonable speculation. I believe that in regards to the wars, it
is a likely conclusion from comparing Ezekiel 37-38 and Zechariah 14 that there will be two different Tribulation wars.

In the first war, which Israel wins, the advancing armies do
not get very far into the land of Israel before they are defeated. I
know one prophet of God who saw it in terms of a volcanic erup-
tion upon the northern armies of Gog and Magog. When he was
visiting Israel, he asked his tour guide, "Are these mountains volcanic?" He was told they were.

A different war comes at the end in Zechariah 14. At that
time all nations will gather together against Jerusalem, and half
the city will go into exile. In the earlier invasion, the armies don't
even get near Jerusalem. In this invasion, they all gather around
Jerusalem, and it looks like Israel is to be completely defeated. It
is because of the outcome of the earlier war that Keith sees the

Jewish people coming back to faith in God. However, he sees it issuing in an orthodox Jewish view. People could be deceived. Even the elect could be deceived. Even Gentiles may believe in orthodox Judaism.

Do I believe there will be a Tribulation temple, that the orthodox will have that kind of victory and control? I don't know. It is not an unlikely scenario; it is possible. If it happens, you read it here first. If it does not happen, that's okay too because it is not something we are saying can be proven by the Word of God. We must make distinctions between those things that are absolute, primary, and clearly establishable by the Word and those which are not, but likely possibilities.

A Broad Summary of the Last Days

I believe what we have laid out in preceding chapters is a correct understanding of the Last Days. The broad summary of what we believe about those days is trustworthy. *It will prepare us for understanding the Book of Revelation.*

- We believe that the Last Days is the last great witness of the Body of believers.
- We believe that the Body of believers will be here throughout the Last Days until near the end of the Tribulation.
- We believe that in these Last Days, in the battles, warfares, and persecutions, the Body of believers will be restored to unity and glory. There will be a worldwide people, either all of the people of God or a remnant of the people of God, which come into the unity and power of the John 17 prayer of Jesus.
- We believe that this body will have a great effect in witnessing to the nation of Israel.

- We believe that in the Last Days the saved remnant of Israel will be reestablished. This remnant is part of the body and still recognizably part of Israel (Jewry). This remnant of Israel will be part of the Last Days witness to Israel.

- We believe that the Last Days will be a time of great kingdom demonstration, a time of persecution, and a time of God's protection.

- We also believe there will be martyrdom. During the battles of the Last Days, great glory will be in evidence from witnessing and the worldwide harvest. It will be the completion of the believers' witness.

- We believe that the saved remnant of Israel, with the Gentile believers, will (after the wars that Keith described) pray Israel into the place where they confess, *"Blessed is He who comes in the name of the Lord."* Both prayer and kingdom demonstration will effect this.

- We believe that the *"Blessed is He who comes in the name of the Lord,"* spoken by Israel's leaders, will lead to the resurrection of the dead (*"What will their acceptance be but life from the dead"*—Rom. 11:15). Israel will see Yeshua, the One whom they pierced.

- We believe that the bowls of God's wrath will then be poured out on the earth. The nations that come against Israel will be defeated. Then, according to Matthew 24 and Revelation 1:7, all nations, or all tribes of the earth will mourn. That mourning of repentance includes all the survivors of God's wrath and the nation of Israel (Zech. 12:11ff; 13:1ff). That repentance will lead to the inauguration of a one-thousand-year period (if you accept it as literal years, and I do).

- We believe there is one more transitional age. It is not the fullness of the ultimate kingdom of the new heavens and new earth, but a breaking in of the kingdom in a very full way so that the conditions predicted by the prophets come into being, even world redemption. *The knowledge of God will cover the earth as the waters cover the sea.* The completion of the Body of believers' intercession and world witness leads to the great judgments and redemptions of God. This in turn leads to the establishment of the reign of Yeshua, which fulfills the promises to Israel.

- We believe the millennial age is an age of the establishment of the biblical feasts. The whole world will connect in some way to that period: a worldwide Sabbath, a worldwide new moon, worldwide Tabernacles, etc.

- We believe that at the end of that age there will be one last rebellion which leads to the final Great White Throne Judgment (Rev. 20).

- We believe that the ultimate "new heavens and new earth" follows. I will explain why in the next chapter.

We see this basic outline of the Last Days as a basis upon which we can engage ourselves in faith activity and worldwide witness. We are a part of its fulfillment. God does not work apart from us. It is not that we humanistically bring it to pass. Neither do we work it out apart from God. God is bringing it about providentially, in His time and in His way, but He is doing it in concert with His people who are willing to intercede to become that Body of John 17:21. So it is a practical eschatology. Thus, we have a broad understanding, an outline of restoration, witness to Israel, persecution, the return of the Lord, and the millennial age.

The Body of Believers Before Yeshua Returns

Now we must fill in some blanks. According to Zechariah 14, during the final invasion of Jerusalem, Jesus stands on the Mount of Olives. After He defeats those nations, all nations that are left celebrate together the Feast of Tabernacles.

Where is the Body of believers, Israel, and the world just before Yeshua returns? My Last Days view of the Church is an eschatology of victory, but premillennial. Namely, the coming of Jesus is the intercessory victory of the Church. As we cry out "maranatha," seeing that world conditions are ready for His return, seeing that we have fulfilled our calling and are a restored Bride made ready for Him, the Rapture will come! It is the next step. What else is left? When we become the restored Bride and complete our witness, it will come. The Rapture is not just something that happens "in the sweet by and by" but is like Enoch's rapture. We will be like Enoch. We must come into a place of readiness to be translated. We will come to that place of readiness as a corporate body. That leads to the Rapture and the resurrection.

Our capstone victory before the Rapture is Israel saying, "*Blessed is He who comes in the name of the Lord.*" It is all intertwined.

The Book of Revelation and Passover-Exodus

I want you to see how this scenario fits into the Book of Revelation. The key to understanding Revelation is the Exodus and Passover. I received this by revelation, but I am very excited that it has scholarly backing. I recently read *Images of the Spirit* by Meredith Kline. It concerns the "glory cloud" and is extremely exciting. In the author's view you must look at the Book of Revelation from the perspective of Passover-Exodus.

The earlier chapters of Revelation are warnings to the churches. Some say those warnings have to do with the various

231

ages of Church history. Some people say the Church today is the
Laodicean church. Maybe prophets are being led to apply those
passages to the Church of this age, but in some ways we are also
the Smyrna church. However, those were real historic congrega-
tions to which God was speaking. Yet the messages to all the
churches have application in all times to various churches.

Daniel and the Book of Revelation

It is common knowledge that the Book of Daniel forms a
background for the Book of Revelation. The symbols and imagery
are pertinent as background material. One of the more important
issues is the interpretation of Daniel 9: 25ff. The very idea of a
seven-year Tribulation, I believe, is derived from a misunderstanding of this section. This misunderstanding is due to not understanding the nature of Hebrew writing—especially when there
is a repetition with an expansion of meaning from one paragraph
to another.

Most agree that Daniel's 70 weeks refer to 490 years of
prophetic time and that the Messiah is cut off after the 69 weeks
or 483 years. However, the interpretation of Daniel's 70th week or
the last seven years of the sequence is at issue. Classical interpretation purports that the Messiah is the one who causes sacrifice
and oblation to cease in the middle of the week. I believe this is an
expansion of the verse concerning the Messiah being cut off, generally after the 69 weeks, but specifically in the middle of the 70th
week. He, the Messiah, confirms the covenant with many for one
week, but in the middle of the week He causes sacrifice and oblation to cease (with regard to its efficacy). This is perfectly in keeping with parallelism and expansion in Hebrew literary style. The
Talmud teaches that the *Yom Kippur* sacrifice was no longer accepted 40 years before the temple was destroyed. This takes us to
the time of the death of Yeshua. Then the apostolic testimony in

Jerusalem offered the covenant to Jerusalem, the New Covenant, for another 3½ years. After this, judgment was decreed. Therefore Daniel's 70th week is past. The Tribulation to come is a different time period at the end of this age and is always described as 3½ years in the Book of Revelation.

I see no warrant for yanking Daniel's 70th week away from the other 69 and placing it some 2,000 years into the future.

Plagues and Judgments

The Book of Revelation is full of the judgments of God. Note that there are twenty-one judgments of God or twenty-one patterns of judgments in the Book of Revelation. Seven is the number of perfection. Three is the number of the triune God. These multiplied equal twenty-one. There are seven seals in Revelation. The seven seals lead to seven *shofarim*, which, in English, are trumpets. The seven trumpets lead to seven bowls of wrath.

In the Exodus, there were ten plagues. In Revelation, we find the Body of believers and especially the Jewish believers, the 144,000, specially protected. I know some people take the 144,000 to be symbolic of the whole Body of believers. I take it to be symbolic of the Jewish remnant that is saved in the Last Days. They are in relationship with the Body of believers in the Book of Revelation. I don't think the Body is gone during this time. The Body of believers is called "the saints" in Revelation. Revelation 7 distinguishes two groups of believers that are contemporary. The first is the Jewish believers from every tribe described as men of virgin purity, a spiritual symbol. The other is those from every tribe and nation that are in a place of special protection in ascended worship. This is the place of the Last Days Body of believers in Revelation. These are not described as martyrs but according to their position as in Ephesians 2:5.

The Mark of the Messiah

The Body of believers, both the Jewish remnant and the rest of the saints, are in a relationship to the world as Israel was to Egypt. The antichrist in Revelation is parallel to Pharaoh. The plagues are not poured out on the believers because they are marked. There is a mark of the beast and also a mark of the Messiah in Revelation. Many people say, "We do not want to go through the time Revelation and experience the plagues God is going to pour out on the earth." However, God's restored body, the Tribulation Body of believers, is like Israel in the land of Goshen. Paul Cain prophesied about there being an AIDS-like plague that will be as contagious as a common cold. If you are a committed part of this John 17 Body of believers of the Last Days, it will not touch you.

You can see what it will be like. God will pour out these plagues on the worldwide Egypt of that day and on the worldwide Pharaoh. He will rip away the veil so that we will not just see it from a natural point of view; there is a spiritual connection even in the present level of plagues. I am not saying that we are in the Revelation period yet. However, the Book of Revelation is a manual of spiritual warfare for all ages. The plagues were poured out on Egypt but not on the land of Goshen. Wherever the Body of believers or an expression of that restored Bride is, there will be a land of Goshen.

Plagues and the Hardening of Hearts

The plagues should lead people to repent. However, what do you find when you read about the seals being opened, the trumpets blowing, the plagues on earth, the fire, and the blood-red seas? Hearts are hardened. Pharaoh, after the plagues were lifted, hardened his heart. What did he do to the people of Israel? He intensified his persecution. We will not experience the plagues of God.

234

We are God's people, but we do have to deal with the persecution of the Last Days Pharaoh or the antichrist, just as Israel did with Pharaoh. Incidentally, you may notice that some of the plagues seem to be the same kinds of plagues as those of Egypt but raised to a higher level of intensity. Revelation describes plagues of insects and water turning to blood. That sounds like the Exodus, doesn't it?

The antichrist is truly foreshadowed by Pharaoh. God pours out a plague. Antichrist hardens his heart just as in the Exodus days. He persecutes. God pours out another plague. Many even say to the rocks and stones, "Fall on us," but they don't repent. Just like the Egyptians, they harden their hearts. Ultimately that succession of plagues and our worldwide witness lead to a parallel to the Exodus through the sea. What happened when the plagues were over? One last outpouring of God's wrath occurred. How was the wrath of God poured out on the Egyptians? It was poured out after Israel escaped through the sea. The sea returned and covered the army of Egypt.

The Escape Through the Glory Cloud

In the Last Days, as I see the scenario in the Book of Revelation, when the people of God are no longer on the earth, God can finally pour out the bowls of wrath that are so extraordinary. Goshens will protect us from the earlier plagues, but we will not be there for the bowls of wrath. We will be on the other side looking back at the armies of the antichrist drowning in the bowls of wrath. Then we will come with the Messiah to defeat the forces of the enemy and to rule and reign. First the veil will open between Heaven and earth, and we will go through it to the other side. Then will come the last judgments. I want to show you explicitly how the Book of Revelation fits into this scenario. It will help you to understand the big picture.

The Sealed of God

After this I saw four angels standing at the four corners of the earth, holding back the four winds of the earth to prevent any wind from blowing on the land or on the sea or on any tree. Then I saw another angel coming up from the east, having the seal of the living God. He called out in a loud voice to the four angels who had been given power to harm the land and the sea: "Do not harm the land or the sea or the trees until we put a seal on the foreheads of the servants of our God." Then I heard the number of those who were sealed: 144,000 from all the tribes of Israel.   Revelation 7:1-4

These servants of God are sealed from experiencing the judgments or plagues that come upon the earth. After this comes the description of the saints from all tribes and nations, a multitude that no one can number. They are before Him in worship.

The Plagues

Let us look at some of the plagues.

The first angel sounded his trumpet, and there came hail and fire mixed with blood, and it was hurled down upon the earth. A third of the earth was burned up, a third of the trees were burned up, and all the green grass was burned up.   Revelation 8:7

The second angel sounded his trumpet, and something like a huge mountain, all ablaze, was thrown into the sea. A third of the sea turned into blood, a third of the living creatures in the sea died, and a third of the ships were destroyed.   Revelation 8:8-9

This plague is parallel to the Nile turning into blood.

*The fourth angel sounded his trumpet, and a third of the
sun was struck, a third of the moon, and a third of the
stars, so that a third of them turned dark. A third of the
day was without light, and also a third of the night.*

Revelation 8:12

This plague is parallel to darkness in the land of Egypt.

*And out of the smoke locusts came down upon the earth
and were given power like that of scorpions of the earth.*

Revelation 9:3

This is parallel to the plague of locusts in the land of Egypt.

The Seventh Trumpet

Chapter 11 is very significant. I believe the seventh trumpet
of the Book of Revelation is the same as the last trumpet of First
Corinthians 15 and the trumpet of God when the dead rise in
First Thessalonians 4:16. What happens when the trumpet sounds?
We are raised, incorruptible. The dead in Messiah rise first, and we
that are alive shall be caught up, raptured, together with them in the
clouds, and so will we ever be with the Lord. Will we just stay there
in the cloud? No, we will come back with Him to put down His enemies and to rule and reign. We will be raised to a higher level of
rulership, fulfilling the purposes of God for us as a people.

*The seventh angel sounded his trumpet, and there were
loud voices in heaven which said: "The kingdom of the
world has become the kingdom of our Lord and of his
Christ, and he will reign forever and ever." And the
twenty-four elders, who were seated on their thrones before God, fell on their faces and worshiped God, saying: "We give thanks to you, Lord God Almighty, the One
who is and who was, because you have taken your great
power and have begun to reign. The nations were angry;*

237

*and your wrath has come. The time has come for judg-
ing the dead, and for rewarding your servants the
prophets and your saints and those who reverence your
name, both small and great—and for destroying those
who destroy the earth."* Revelation 11:15-18

All of this started after the seventh shofar sounded. The seventh seal opens the seven trumpets. The seventh trumpet leads to the bowls of wrath. Out of the trumpet comes the seven bowls.

The Woman and the Child

Before the bowls, we read an historical scenario which is not difficult to interpret. It is an excursus or a parenthesis in the events. This is the birth of Jesus from Israel, the woman.

*She gave birth to a son, a male child, who will rule all
the nations with an iron scepter. And her child was
snatched up to God and to his throne.* Revelation 12:5

This is the resurrection and ascension of Jesus.

*The woman fled into the desert to a place prepared for
her by God, where she might be taken care of for 1,260
days.* Revelation 12:6

In verse 5, the woman, Israel, flees into the wilderness and is yet protected by God in the Last Days. I think you can apply it to the general preservation of Israel throughout history, but it especially applies to the last Tribulation, which is described as about three and a half years.

*When the dragon saw that he had been hurled to the
earth, he pursued the woman who had given birth to the
male child. The woman was given the two wings of a
great eagle, so that she might fly to the place prepared
for her in the desert, where she would be taken care of
for a time, times and half a time, out of the serpent's*

238

*reach. Then from his mouth the serpent spewed water
like a river, to overtake the woman and sweep her away
with the torrent.* Revelation 12:13-15

God's protection of Israel is seen even more explicitly here.

*But the earth helped the woman by opening its mouth
and swallowing the river that the dragon had spewed
out of his mouth.* Revelation 12:16

There is a satanic rage against the Jewish people. Hitler was
from satan. What does satan do after his rage against Israel is
thwarted? He goes to make war with the rest of her offspring. The
Book of Revelation provides us with a glorious perspective, that
the Body of believers is the offspring of Israel. We are the spiritual seed of Israel. The whole body, Jew and Gentile, is of Israel.

The Antichrist and the False Prophet

Revelation 13 is another excursus giving a picture of the Last
Days and of the antichrist and the false prophet who leads false religion in the Last Days.

*And I saw a beast coming out of the sea. He had ten
horns and seven heads, with ten crowns on his horns,
and on each head a blasphemous name.* Revelation 13:1

This gives us a picture of the Antichrist coming out of the
sea. The sea is symbolic of people in prophetic literature. The antichrist, the beast, rises out of the people as does the false prophet.
The antichrist will have his righthand prophet, just as a king had
his righthand prophet in ancient days.

Remember, the seventh trumpet has sounded. We have not
yet seen the bowls of wrath. What we are seeing is a flashback of
the total picture. We see false political power and false religion
growing until it controls all of life. World conditions even now reflect these possibilities.

The Harvest of Deliverance

I looked, and there before me was a white cloud, and seated on the cloud was one "like a son of man" with a crown of gold on his head and a sharp sickle in his hand. Then another angel came out of the temple and called in a loud voice to him who was sitting on the cloud, "Take your sickle and reap, because the time to reap has come, for the harvest of the earth is ripe." So he who was seated on the cloud swung his sickle over the earth, and the earth was harvested.

Revelation 14:14-16

This reads much like Matthew 24. Some of this is parallel to what happened in first-century Israel, but there are differences. How do we deal with that? I believe that prophecy which ultimately looks toward the end has one meaning but different times of partial manifestation. You see it in different ages of history. Matthew 24 was partly fulfilled in the first century, but the tribulations of the Last Days in Matthew 24 are ultimately to be seen in the final Last Days. The thrust of that prophecy concerns the coming of the Lord in the Last Days Tribulation. I believe we are near this time.

We read that the earth is to be harvested in Revelation 14:14ff as well. You will notice, as we look at Revelation 14, two different harvests. Some people think that when the witnesses of Revelation 11 go up to Heaven it is symbolic of the Rapture and that this is a repeat vision. The witnesses are seen as the Church. I think the witnesses are representative of Last Days prophets and possibly two specific prophet leaders. I see this as an earlier resurrection preceding the Rapture. The first harvest in Revelation is the harvest of the saints, as described in the above quote from Revelation 14:14-16, 1 Thessalonians 4:16-17, and Matthew 24. This is what some have called the Rapture.

The Messiah comes on the cloud. In Revelation we are seeing into the cloud. The cloud, I believe, is the glory cloud of the ancient tabernacle. It is a manifestation of God's glory, a plane of transition between this world and the heavenly world. You look and see inside that cloud, as Ezekiel did, and see it is not just a cloud. You see cherubim and wheels within wheels. What do you ultimately see? It may appear to be just a cloud when you are at a distance from it, but the cloud is really the entryway into Heaven. You can see into Heaven when you are in the cloud.

Ezekiel saw the cloud with more definition. Throughout the Book of Revelation, John is seeing into the glory cloud that was with the children of Israel in the Exodus. As he looked into the glory cloud, he could see the things Ezekiel saw. He saw the altar, the angels, and the throne. That is also what Ezekiel saw in the cloud. The first harvest is the Rapture of the saints into the glory cloud. Then comes the harvest for wrath.

The Harvest for Wrath

The second harvest is a gathering of the nations for judgment. We read:

Still another angel, who had charge of the fire, came from the altar and called in a loud voice to him who had the sharp sickle, "Take your sharp sickle and gather the clusters of grapes from the earth's vine, because its grapes are ripe." Revelation 14:18

All the plagues of Revelation to this point did not constitute "the wrath of God."

The angel swung his sickle on the earth, gathered its grapes and threw them into the great winepress of God's wrath. Revelation 14:19

The wrath of God over the earth sheds so much blood it would fill a great depth if it were collected in one place. In this second harvest an angel swings his sickle and reaps the earth for the wrath of God. The wheat will be gathered, and the chaff will be burned.

The Bowls of the Wrath of God

When the events of Revelation 15 and 16 come upon the earth, I don't believe we will be here any longer. Metaphorically we will be on the other side of the sea looking at the drowning of Pharaoh's troops. Revelation 16 presents the bowls of God's wrath. I believe this will happen very quickly, perhaps from one to three weeks. In Revelation 17 and 18 we see the destruction of the harlot, the destruction of the beast, and the destruction of the Babylonian system. This again is a larger picture of Last Days opposition as in Revelation 13. It is another parenthesis. I believe the bowls of wrath of Revelation 16, the winepress of wrath of Revelation 14, and the Revelation 19 winepress of wrath will happen together when the armies of the world invade Israel.

Out of this mouth comes a sharp sword with which to strike down the nations.

What does Isaiah 11 say about the Messiah? *"He shall smite the earth with the rod of His mouth."* Revelation 19 says the same thing in different terms. It says that Jesus will *"tread the winepress of God's wrath."*

The Messiah and His Armies

The armies of Heaven follow Him. This might be angelic armies, but, according to the prophets, the Lord shall come with all His saints or holy ones, which could be the Body of believers. This is the picture of Zechariah 14 and 1 Thessalonians 4:17. What do we see? We see that the Messiah comes and stands on the Mount of Olives. The Lord and His saints go forth to fight the two beasts and the armies that come upon Jerusalem. We read the same events in Revelation 19 and Zechariah 14. Of the birds of prey we read,

> *So that you may eat the flesh of kings, generals, and mighty men, of horses and their riders, and the flesh of all people, free and slave, small and great.*
>
> Revelation 19:18

What does God say in Isaiah 25-27, known as "the little apocalypse of Isaiah"? He says that on this mountain He will make a feast and destroy the veil that is over the eyes of all nations. The veil is the deception of satan. This great manifestation of the Messiah with the sons of God in Revelation finally rips aside the veil that is over the nations. The beast's defeat by the Messiah and His saints ends the deception. After that battle, as we read in Zechariah 14, the nations left from that destruction will go up year after year and celebrate the feast of Succot. *"In that day the Lord will be One and His Name One over all the earth. The Lord shall be King over all the earth"* (Zech. 14:9ff. NKJV).

Redemption and Wrath Together

I believe that if you look carefully at all the passages you will see God's redemption and wrath come together for His people. The wrath of God does not fall on the Jewish people who were not yet saved, but who corporately, through their leaders, say, *"Blessed is He who comes in the name of the Lord."* That portion of Israel that is not believing before the Rapture, but is part of the corporate confession, goes into the millennial age with the other nations. We who are resurrected establish the millennial kingdom age and delegate to authorities among the earthly people.

Zechariah describes the Body of believers and the world situation before the Messiah returns.

A day of the Lord is coming when your plunder will be divided among you. I will gather all the nations to Jerusalem to fight against it; the city will be captured, the houses ransacked, and the women raped. Half of the city will go into exile, but the rest of the people will not be taken from the city. Zechariah 14:1-2

Remember, First Thessalonians says, "*You are not in darkness that that day should overtake you as a thief.*" We are to watch. When we see this invasion, we will know this is it!

We are one of the streams of the restored worldwide Body of believers of the Last Days. We are witnessing and gaining a harvest. Yet we are also seeing Last Days events. People are experiencing plagues; others are part of the great harvest. Where do you suppose the harvest comes from? The harvest comes from those people who want to be healed from the plagues. Who can heal them? You can. The Book of Revelation brings out both plagues and harvests. People can join the Goshen protected company. After all the plagues of Egypt, what did Pharaoh do? Did he let Israel go? No, he went after Israel. He followed them into the sea. The earth is experiencing all the plagues, but the nations of the earth do not say, "We should turn to God, look at all the miracles!" I believe in the victory of God's people, but I have a problem with the scenario that says, "Without the coming of the Lord and the revelation of His saints, we will win the whole world to Jesus because we have the Spirit."

Do We Take Over Before Jesus Comes?

Jesus, when He was on earth, could not win all the Pharisees, Sadducees, and scribes. The apostles could not win Israel to God. Though we will have the fullness of God's power, not everybody will fall down and repent. That is the problem with postmillennialism. There will also be false miracles. Pharaoh's magicians were able to imitate the plagues, but they couldn't remove the plagues! The antichrist and false prophet will do signs and wonders (Rev. 13). We will know in the midst of these plagues, in the midst of the miracles, in the midst of the worldwide harvest, in the midst of the supernatural protection, that we are in the last of the Last Days. We will press the issue of world evangelism and Jewish evangelism that this period might end. This will be a most difficult period, yet the most glorious period for the Body of believers until the Rapture. We should look forward to entering it.

The Plagues and the Final Invasion of Israel

What happens next? All those plagues come and the world-Pharaoh does not repent. Instead, he pursues Israel. He leads a world invasion. The nations of Europe have come together under a unified money system. Things are happening that have never happened before. I do believe there will be some type of world government, but more loose than in past empires.

At the end of all the plagues, the antichrist invades Israel. This is the point at which we believers realize what time it is. The World Series score in the seventh game is: the devil, 6; the people of God, 3 (from an earthly point of view; see the end of the chapter for the conclusion of the World Series analogy). Think of how it will be to the Jew. If Keith's scenario about orthodoxy is true, that the Jewish people will again believe for the protection of God, the question will be: Where is God now? Israel has seen the victory of Ezekiel 38, but now the nations invade and it appears that all is lost. What a devastating time! Half the city is in exile; the women are raped. This has never happened before without leading to the utter destruction of Jerusalem. (It happened twice before to total destruction under the Babylonians and the Romans.) This time, for the first time in history, Israel will not be totally destroyed. However, she will suffer serious destruction.

The Great Birth Pangs of Intercession

What has to happen next? The leaders of Israel must come together. Whether it is those left in the city or those outside the city, the leaders will have to come together. Where will the Church be? Crying out in intercession, experiencing birth pains for the Messiah. Women who have experienced the pangs of birth tell us that nothing compares to it. On that day even the men will be in labor and intercession. We will be crying out, "Lord God, this is it; save Your people Israel; come Lord! Let them say the confession!" The leadership of Israel will ask, "What will we do? This is worse than Hitler; it is the end of our Zionist dream; the state of Israel is about to be destroyed. It's all over." Somebody will respond, "Yes, but the believers in Jesus who are Jewish told us this would happen."

Israel Calls on Jesus to Save Them

This is why it is important for us to publicize the basic events of the Last Days to Jewish people, even if they don't believe us. We must place the information in their hands. Someone must be able to say, "The messianic Jews have told us that this would happen."

"Yes, and the worldwide Church is standing with us. They have been suffering persecution under the same forces," someone will add. Finally the Church gets it right and stands with Israel!

Then somebody will say, "You know, they have been saying to us that our trouble began back in the first century. The temple doors opened of their own accord showing that God was finished with the temple. The scarlet cord that annually on the Day of Atonement turned white miraculously no longer turned white. All this was forty years before the temple was destroyed. What happened forty years before the temple was destroyed? Jesus died. Is it possible we missed it with regards to Yeshua?"

246

Then somebody may say, "What is it the believers have been saying we must say if we are in this position? *Blessed is He who comes in the name of the Lord"?*

One will say, "I don't know, we have never done that before."

Another will say, "What do we have to lose? If He comes, He saves us; if He doesn't, it can't make things worse than they are right now."

As this conversation takes place, the Body of the Messiah is in great prayer.

Finally, the leaders will say, "Let's try it. Let's call out to Yeshua and see if He will save us, and see if He is the Messiah."

Then that gathered leadership, what I call a reconstituted Sanhedrin, reverses the decision of the first century and says, *Baruch Haba Bashem Adoni.*

The Church is crying, "Maranatha! Come, Lord." Then it all comes together!

Critical Mass in the Spirit

The Body of believers will be at a critical mass point. There is nothing left for us but the Rapture. For the spiritual explosion to take place, one ingredient must be added to our critical mass point. That is Israel's confession. When Israel confesses the Messiah, **B-O-O-M!** And it all happens between verses 2 and 3 of Zechariah 14. His feet will stand on the Mount of Olives, and from there the Lord will go forth and fight against those nations. The bowls-of-wrath period of Revelation 16 and 19 follows.

> *On that day his feet will stand on the Mount of Olives, east of Jerusalem, and the Mount of Olives will be split in two from east to west, forming a great valley, with half of the mountain moving north and half moving south. You will flee by my mountain valley, for it will*

extend to Azel. You will flee as you fled from the earth-quake in the days of Uzziah King of Judah. Then the LORD my God will come, and all the holy ones with him. On that day there will be no light, no cold or frost. It will be a unique day, without daytime or nighttime— a day known to the LORD. When evening comes, there will be light. On that day living water will flow out from Jerusalem, half to the eastern sea and half to the western sea, in summer and in winter. The LORD will be king over the whole earth. On that day there will be one LORD, and his name the only name. Zechariah 14:4-9

Do you see the power of this? Do you see what God has ordained for His people and for Israel? Can you see why Paul said it is through the mercies shown to you that Israel will receive mercy? *"What will their acceptance be but life from the dead!"* How much more shall their acceptance be indeed!

Worldwide Repentance

After Messiah returns with His saints and all the earth sees Him, the whole earth mourns (Matt. 24; Rev. 1:7). Israel repents; the nations repent. The Body doesn't have to repent. Our repenting will already have taken place. We will have met the Lord in the air. We will see Him and come back with Him in a very brief time sequence. These are the events we anticipate in the Last Days.

Carrying our baseball analogy a bit further, let us be sure that the Series goes seven games and that we have three runs and three on base in the bottom of the ninth inning. This is our prayer. Then Yeshua, our player-manager, will come to the plate and hit a grand slam home run. The final score will be 7 – 6 (7 being the number of God and 6 the number of the antichrist)!

We have our part to play, but we can only do it through His Spirit in us. However, with only one out to go, it is Jesus Himself who comes to hit the home run!

CHAPTER 9

THE FEASTS, THE LAST DAYS,
AND THE MILLENNIAL AGE

by Daniel Juster

God has hidden, in the Jewish biblical feasts, the predominant themes of the Last Days. The Jewish feasts have never been done away with. They are windows through which to see the purposes of God. They come to their fullness in Yeshua. This is part of the age to come breaking into this age. As we enter more into the Last Days, more of the Kingdom will break in. In the millennial age, when the Kingdom comes in greater fullness, all the feasts will be established!

Passover

Passover is the feast that gives us an understanding of several dimensions. Every feast is overlapping in meaning. None is totally distinct in its meaning. The various feasts say the same thing but with different emphases. The emphases for Passover are blood redemption, the Exodus from Egypt, and the New Year. Therefore, in the prophetic scenario, Passover parallels the last great Tribulation. That is why it is appropriate to teach on the Last Days Tribulation from the Feast of Passover. Passover points prophetically to the Book of Revelation, to the exodus of the Church, Jew and Gentile. Then it points to the regathering of Israel, because in the millennial age (Jer. 16 and 23) it will no longer be said, *"The Lord who brought us out of the land of Egypt, but the Lord who brought us out of all the nations to which He had scattered us—the north, the south, the east and the west.*"

Somebody may ask, "Do you mean that we are not to re-member the Exodus anymore?" No, we will never forget the Exodus from Egypt, but the glory of being regathered and entering into the promise of the millennial age, seeing the fulfillment of the prophets' vision and of world peace will be so much greater! When Passover time comes, it will be said, "*The Lord who brought us out of all the lands to which He had scattered us,*" because we will have seen greater miracles. I don't think we have seen these great miracles yet. Israel's existence is a miracle. The second exodus out of Russia is a miracle. The regathering of the Millennium, however, will make the Exodus look like nothing, and it is proba-bly the greatest miracle to date, except for the resurrection of Jesus.

Firstfruits

The first day after the Sabbath of Passover is the Feast of Firstfruits when the first produce of the land was waved and of-fered to God. Yeshua is the firstfruit of the resurrection. The feast of unleavened bread, therefore, celebrates His resurrection.

Shavuot

The feast of *Shavuot* is the early harvest of wheat and barley. The early spiritual harvest came through the pouring out of the Holy Spirit on *Shavuot* (Pentecost). This is a harvest feast, and it represents a harvest of souls as well. The early harvest always points to the latter harvest. *Shavuot* is always pointing to *Sukkot* (Tabernacles), the latter harvest. *Shavuot* looks toward the ulti-mate outpouring of the Spirit. Peter's quote of Joel was only for a partial breaking in. "*This is that which was spoken by the prophet.*

Old men dreamed dreams. And whosoever will call on the name of the Lord will be saved." The ultimate fulfillment of Pentecost is the millennial age. Just before the millennial age, we will see the full blossoming of the gifts of the Spirit, which have been in the process of restoration to the Church since 1830.

God through His Spirit enables us to keep the law. *Shavuot* is the feast remembering the giving of the Law. Why does God pour out His Spirit on *Shavuot*? Because it is only by the Spirit that we can keep God's Law. We don't do away with the Law. We keep the Law through the Spirit (not as legalism and self-effort).

The Fall Feasts

The fall feasts are especially important because they speak prophetically of the return of Jesus and the establishment of the kingdom.

Rosh Hashanah

The fall feasts begin with *Rosh Hashanah. Rosh Hashanah* is not the correct name. It is really called *Yom Teru'ah* or *Yom Hashofar*. The first name means "the feast of the blowing." The feast is commonly called *Rosh Hashanah* because rabbis calculated that the creation of the world took place and time began with *Rosh Hashanah*, the New Year.

Do I believe that? Probably not, though it is possible. Another reason that date was celebrated as a new year was that there existed already a Middle Eastern new year at that season. In the Bible, it was not called a new year. In Jewish tradition (and I think this tradition is prophetic), the judgments of God are determined between *Yom Hashofar* and *Yom Kippur*. If you have made your peace with God by the Day of Atonement, within the ten days, you will live; if you have not, it will be too late.

If the wrath of God, which is God's judgment, is poured out after the seventh shofar sounds (Rev. 11), that is most interesting. When I think of the shofar, I think of gathering the army of God for war. The shofar blows to gather the saints together. It will blow to gather us to Messiah, and we will become fully like Him—in the Rapture and the resurrection. We shall see Him as He is. We will come with Him, and we will reign with Him! Once the shofar sounds, the saints are raised.

If the literal wrath of God will occur during the eight-day period between *Rosh Hoshanah* and *Yom Kippur*, after the Rapture, this would fit very well. Perhaps for that brief period we will not be visible to the people still on earth as the wrath is poured out. We disappear, but soon we do come back with Him. I don't know the exact time scenario, whether it will be a literal eight days or whether these days are symbolic. When Israel says, "*Blessed is He who comes in the name of the Lord*," the Rapture will take place. There is then an eight-day period on the Jewish calendar between the shofar blast and the Day of Repentance and Atonement.

Yom Kippur (The Day of Atonement)

And I will pour out on the house of David and the inhabitants of Jerusalem a spirit of grace and supplication. They will look on me, the one they have pierced, and they will mourn for him as one mourns for an only child, and grieve bitterly for him as one grieves for a firstborn son. Zechariah 12:10

Mourning and repentance are the themes of Yom Kippur. We read also, in Matthew 24:30, that "*all of the tribes of the earth shall mourn*" when they see Him in the glory cloud. Revelation declares the same thing:

Look, he is coming with the clouds, and every eye will see him, even those who pierced him; and all the peoples of

*the earth will mourn because of him. So shall it be!
Amen.*   Revelation 1:7

The resurrection of *Rosh Hashanah*, followed by the wrath and judgments of God and the deliverance of Israel in Zechariah 14, leads to worldwide mourning. Israel and the nations mourn. Israel's mourning is also representative. I believe that a worldwide *Yom Kippur*, a day of repentance, will occur. Whether it is symbolized by the day of *Yom Kippur*, or whether it actually takes place on that very day, I am not sure. Of that day we read that God will pour out upon the Jewish nation a spirit of grace and supplication, and they will mourn for Him as one mourns for his only son (Zech. 12:10).

Sukkot (Tabernacles)

What happens after *Yom Kippur*? What do Jewish people do after *Yom Kippur*? They go out and build a *sukkah*, a tent dwelling. *Sukkot* is the feast in which we celebrate the fact that God supplies all our needs. Dwelling in booths reminds us of our dependence on God. In Jewish tradition, *Sukkot* is the feast of the establishment of God's worldwide kingdom. The feast of *Sukkot* is an eight-day celebration.

In Zechariah 14 we read that all nations will celebrate the feast of *Sukkot*. The Talmud tractate on *Sukkot*, information on the celebration, clarifies the actions of Yeshua during *Sukkot*: *"I am the light of the world,"* He said. This was the time when the great lamps were lit in the court of the temple. The light was described as awesomely glorious. This was also the feast for the taking of water from the pool of Siloam and pouring it out in the temple before God. Yeshua in this context said that He is the water of life for anyone who thirsts. This probably relates to a water-pouring ceremony during *Sukkot*. The great commentary on the Gospel of John by Raymond Brown brings this out forcefully.

The Talmud also indicates that the feast of *Sukkot* was the time when the nation of Israel engaged in priestly intercessory sacrifice for all other nations of the world. In Jewish reckoning, because of Genesis 10, there are seventy nations. Therefore, there were seventy sacrifices offered for the nations during *Sukkot*. We read in a *Sukkot* context (Zech. 14:9) that *"the Lord will be one and His name one in all the earth."*

Sukkot prophetically testifies that God provides for all our needs. The theme is the final harvest: The whole world will be harvested into the Kingdom of God. Yeshua is the firstfruits, we are like the first harvest, but Sukkot is the whole world harvested into the Kingdom of God. There will be worldwide prosperity; reaping and planting will overtake each other.

Sukkot, therefore, is the eight-day celebration of the worldwide coronation of the King on the earth, the worldwide acceptance of and exaltation of Yeshua. It is the eight-day feast in which He will come into His own possession. Surely He has already been exalted, but *Sukkot* will be the acknowledgment of His Kingship over the earth and the worldwide celebration of His Kingship.

Having gone through *Yom Kippur*, the world can celebrate *Sukkot*. Having gone through the Feast of Repentance, they can enter into the feast of the celebration of the King and His Bride-Queen, the Body of believers. That is what *Sukkot* is all about; it will be celebrated every year. I believe *Sukkot* is the marriage supper of the Lamb and the inauguration of the King and His Queen, the first millennial *Sukkot*.

The Millennial Age

That leads us to the question of the millennial age. Some people have a problem understanding the millennial age. I believe that the people remaining on earth (those who are not resurrected) will make up a people of God in that age. They will be filled with the Spirit, and they will walk in all the promises of God. The reason some people have a problem believing in a literal Millennium is that to the human mind it seems foolish that resurrected and non-resurrected people could work together. It seems odd that after Jesus finally comes we don't immediately enter into the new heavens and new earth, and that after Jesus reigns on earth for a thousand years there will be one more rebellion against Him. That is unthinkable to some people.

This is the reason why amillennialists look at the thousand years as symbolic of the reign of believers in Heaven, the reign of those at this present time who have died and gone to Heaven, or somehow our present reign on earth, but not a literal Millennium.

Why a Literal Millennium Makes Sense

First, there is precedent in the Scriptures for resurrected and non-resurrected people being together. For example, Yeshua was with His disciples for forty days. He appeared and disappeared. I do believe that is the model for the Millennium. The resurrected saints are not always here dwelling in earthly houses. I believe that we will come in and out of the earth with Him. We will be on the scene more in the beginning of the Millennium and less at the end of the Millennium. Elijah and Moses were able to interact with Yeshua and His three disciples on the Mount of Transfiguration, though they were not in earthly bodies.

Secondly, heavenly beings and earthly beings interacting is often found in the Bible. I don't see any problem with that.

The Millennial Age Parallels the Pre-Flood Age

Thirdly, the millennial age is a necessary transition to the new heavens and new earth because God works in a process of restoration, turning things back toward paradise, through the pre-flood stage of humanity. If you look at the fall of Adam, a restoration points to a millennial age. Revelation 20 fits Isaiah's description of an age in which a person who dies at one hundred years old is considered accursed to have died in childhood! If death at one hundred is a childhood death, what do you think the life span will be? Man will achieve longevity, perhaps nearly a thousand-year life span.

Further, Isaiah describes the age as one of marriages and joyous births of children. Therefore, I believe the millennial age is parallel to the pre-flood stage of human existence. Before the flood took place, human beings lived more than nine hundred years. Noah was six hundred when he built the ark. That is a Kingdom breakthrough. We are already beginning to see some signs of the Millennium breaking forth among believers, even on this side of the resurrection, as they walk in wholeness or healing.

What happened to man? He was living a long life then started to go downhill. A great cataclysmic flood came. After the flood men still lived to be 175, but life expectancy continued to decline. By the time of David, "three score and ten" was the expected life span. The same sin that brought on the great flood caused man to live a shorter life. After the judgment of the flood, God said He would never destroy the earth by flood again. If restoration is reversing this process, the parallel to the flood is the wrath of God being poured out. The wrath of God's judgment reverses the trend begun with the flood. Those who enter the Millennium without translated bodies can recapture the longevity of the pre-flood age. The believers who walk in healing now are a prophetic foreshadowing of this longevity.

Living Out Faith

Why is it that they will live so long? Because when satan has been bound, the whole earth will accept Yeshua, and we as resurrected saints will be ruling. If satan is not there tempting the human race, people will be able to live fully on biblical health. They will be able to believe for their healing; they will be able to believe for their prosperity; and they will be able to walk in all the promises of God in an earthly existence. This will demonstrate the principles of God's Law and promises as true. We need a full earthly demonstration of the fact that God's Law brings prosperity in an earthly plane. You have to prove it on an earthly plane, not a heavenly plane. We, the saints of this age, will have already been translated or resurrected. God wants to demonstrate the principles of faith and His Law. Remember, the goal of the New Covenant is not to do away with the Law, but the empowerment of the Spirit to fulfill the Law.

The Law of God Established

In Isaiah 2, we read that on that day the Law will go forth from Zion and the word of the Lord will go forth from Jerusalem. The Messiah will not rest until He establishes Jerusalem as a praise on the earth. The nations will come under His Law. This will not be the reestablishment of the Mosaic covenant literally, but Moses applied to the millennial age with the millennial temple— as is appropriate to a New Covenant age. The Millennium is a New Covenant age! The temple will reflect the reality of Yeshua's redemption; it will be the full living out, in an earthly stage, of the New Covenant. We will secure the world as His resurrected people. We will appear to the people on earth. We will choose people to be earthly leaders. Israel will be the head of all nations. Jewish designates will be represented in every nation because the Jewish people will teach the world the Law of God. Resurrected people will be present too and will establish Isaiah's order, where the knowledge of the Lord will cover the earth as the waters cover the sea (Isa. 11). The earth will experience beneficial climate change, the curse of shortened life will be removed, and natural prosperity will abound. Those people who repent at the beginning of the Millennium will come into the fullness of God and live out the Law by faith. They will follow God.

The Test at the End of the Millennium

What happens at the end of the Millennium? Everyone who entered the millennial age at its beginning, I believe, will die. Natural death finally does take its toll, just as it did with our long-living ancestors. There must then be a test for those who were born during the Millennium. None of those who saw the glorious beginning of the age will still be alive. Those new souls remaining must decide if they will submit to God's authority or fall under deception to establish their own authority.

As the millennial age goes on, those of us who were resurrected will pull back from our direct rule and turn it over to delegated rulers. As the age goes on, we pull back more and more. So there must be one more test. Who will people obey? What will their hearts be like? Will they be born again? They will have been taught by their parents, but their parents will be gone. Now there are rebellious children on earth.

The Last Rebellion

Will most of the people remaining on earth be young people? Perhaps. All those who remain will be tested. Satan will be loosed to try and delude these people. Will they choose God or not? We are told that many people will rebel against Israel, and Messiah will have to come and put down the last rebellion.

The Great White Throne Judgment

This will lead to the Great White Throne Judgment. Some people have thought that all who are judged at the Great White Throne Judgment go to hell. That would only be the case if nobody were saved in the Millennium. Revelation 20 says, *"If anyone's name was not found written in the book of life, he was cast into the lake of fire.*" The implication here is that there will be people whose names are written in the Lamb's book of life. We are not part of that judgment. We have already been resurrected and are reigning with the Lord. We will already have appeared before the judgment of the Messiah (1 Cor. 5). At the later Great White Throne Judgment all those who were saved during the millennial age become joined to us. They become resurrected and form part of the Bride with us. The lost from all ages will be cast into the lake of fire.

A Summary of God's Plan

God's judgment is final; our witness is almost complete. World history has seen the decline of man after the fall. Man, God's glorious creation, declined until he lived only a short seventy-year span. Yeshua, our Head, came to earth as a man to redeem fallen man. He has made it possible for us to be one with Him. He is our representative. We will be with Him. All of this long course of world history has been recorded on God's everlasting video-tapes. It records the rise of the Body of believers out of the ashes of decline and its gradual restoration to fullness in the Last Days until the return of Yeshua.

In that day, the last chapter will be written. The final drama will be played out. The ultimate truth of all of God's laws and principles will be established. There will be an age in which earthly people can live by faith in all of God's laws and promises. Then a new age will begin for us all, the age of the new heavens and new earth where we will dwell with our God. We will praise Him in the new Jerusalem, the temple that comes down from above. This is the final restoration as seen in Revelation 22. We will, at last, be restored to Eden, to eat of the tree of life forever. We will have more than we lost in Eden. As the flood initiated a decline in age, the wrath of God and repentance initiate the restoration of longevity. Then the last judgment at the end of the Millennium restores paradise, the new Jerusalem.

Clarifying Confusion on the Millennium

The prophets did not write a book of systematic theology. Isaiah talks about people living to great age and at the same time calls it a new heavens and new earth (Isa. 66). The millennial age is a new heavens and new earth, but it is not the ultimate new heavens and new earth talked about in Revelation 21. Isaiah saw a new heavens and new earth with people living to old age and dying, people marrying and having children. Perhaps he merges the Millennium with the ultimate new heavens and new earth because he does not yet distinguish them. Maybe "new heavens and new earth" should not be taken as such a technically precise concept. Surely the Millennium, compared to this age, is a new heaven and new earth. The new heavens and new earth in Revelation 21–22 is the ultimate. Some believe that the longevity mentioned is just symbolic of eternal life. If that is so, what does the dying mean? Is that symbolic of eternal life? Why is there still a seed-time and a harvest and marriages and births? Are these all symbolic of eternal life? Unless the text specifically tells me they are symbolic, I cannot receive them as such. There is a difference between everlasting life and a long, limited life!

Some say the reason the prophets talked as if there would be an earthly Millennium was so that simple people could understand eternal life. That is not true. The ancients already had the tradition of the tree of life. They knew that if Adam and Eve had eaten of the tree of life (instead of the tree of the knowledge of good and evil), they would have had everlasting life. If, in describing the Millennium, the prophets were trying to describe everlasting life instead of earthly longevity, they could have said, "everlasting life through eating of the tree of life." Everyone would have understood them. If they meant "eternal life," they should have said "eternal life." This leads us to a pre-millennial or literal millennium view.

The New Jerusalem

One of the seven angels who had the seven bowls full of the seven last plagues came and said to me, "Come, I will show you the bride, the wife of the Lamb." And he carried me away in the Spirit to a mountain great and high, and showed me the Holy City, Jerusalem, coming down out of heaven from God. It shone with the glory of God, and its brilliance was like that of a very precious jewel, like a jasper, clear as crystal. It had a great, high wall with twelve gates, and with twelve angels at the gates. On the gates were written the names of the twelve tribes of Israel. There were three gates on the east, three on the north, three on the south, and three on the west. The wall of the city had twelve foundations, and on them were the names of the twelve apostles of the Lamb. I did not see a temple in the city, because the Lord God Almighty and the Lamb are its temple. The city does not need the sun or the moon to shine on it, for the glory of God gives it light, and the Lamb is its lamp. The nations will walk by its light and the kings of the earth will bring their splendor into it. Revelation 21:9-14,22-24

The new Jerusalem that comes out of Heaven is both the people and the city, the bride of the Lamb. The foundation stones of the city bear the names of the twelve Jewish apostles. Its gates bear the names of the twelve tribes of Israel. All of God's people have their roots in Israel and will dwell forever in the glory of the City of God. We will live in His presence forever! Glory to God!

He is restoring that which is lost. Human history passed through the stages of paradise in Eden, to pre-flood longevity, to post-flood brevity of life, to the restoration of healing through Yeshua, and will yet pass through a restoration (after the wrath of God) to longevity of life in the Millennium. A better paradise than the first will be established, the new heavens and new earth.

We will be with Yeshua forever. Praise be His name! We will live in an eternal human community in the love of God! Indeed, God will preserve a variety of peoples to enrich the everlasting kingdom. He values varieties of cultures and peoples. He is a God who creates many personalities; we are not all to be the same.

May we live so as to "hasten the day" of His coming! *"Maranatha! Even so come, Lord Jesus!"*

THE DECLINE AND RESTORATION OF MAN

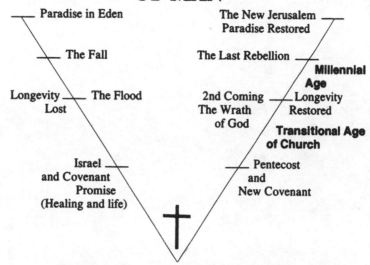

THE DECLINE AND RESTORATION OF THE CHURCH

KEITH INTRATER & DAN JUSTER

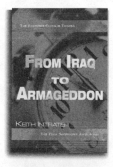

FROM IRAQ TO ARMAGEDDON
Keith Intrater

Never was a book more needed to unravel the controversies surrounding the conflicts in the Middle East. *From Iraq to Armageddon* is an in-depth analysis of end-time prophecy concerning this dangerous region of the world. Messianic Jewish scholar Keith Intrater answers many intriguing questions about prophecy and the Middle East.
ISBN 0-7684-2186-1

COVENANT RELATIONSHIPS
Keith Intrater

This is a handbook on the biblical principles of integrity and loyalty. it lays important foundations for congregational health and right spiritual attitudes. Topics include relationships, the meaning of life, how a blood covenant works, financial accountability, and more!
ISBN 0-914903-71-3

ISRAEL, THE CHURCH, AND THE LAST DAYS
Keith Intrater & Dan Juster

What part does Israel play in the last days? Is the Kingdom now? Is it future? Or is it both? These and other questions are answered with scriptural clarity as the authors delve into this timely and prophetic topic.
ISBN 0-7684-2187-X

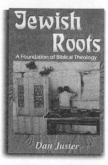

JEWISH ROOTS
Dan Juster

A Messianic Jewish scholar, Dan Juster is well able to discuss many difficult questions that face Messianic Jews. From examining God's call on Israel to Paul and the Law, Dan Juster presents a solid foundation for biblical theology that includes its *Jewish Roots*.
ISBN 1-56043-142-3

Available at your local Christian bookstore.

For more information and sample chapters, visit www.destinyimage.com

Additional copies of this book and other
book titles from DESTINY IMAGE are
available at your local bookstore.

For a complete list of our titles,
visit us at www.destinyimage.com
Send a request for a catalog to:

Destiny Image₍ᵣ₎ Publishers, Inc.
P.O. Box 310
Shippensburg, PA 17257-0310

*"Speaking to the Purposes of God for This
Generation and for the Generations to Come"*